Ralf Vogt
"Beseelbare" Therapy Objects

edition psychosozial

Ralf Vogt

"Beseelbare" Therapy Objects

Psychoanalytical-Activity-Specific Approach
in a trauma- and body-oriented psychotherapy

Translated by Anni Pott
Proofreading and editoral work by Paula M. Niemietz

Psychosozial-Verlag

Original title:
Ralf Vogt:
Beseelbare Therapieobjekte.
Strukturelle Handlungsinszenierungen in einer
körper- und traumaorientierten Psychotherapie
© 2004 by Psychosozial-Verlag

Bibliografische Information der Deutschen Nationalbibliothek
Die Deutsche Nationalbibliothek verzeichnet diese Publikation in der Deutschen
Nationalbibliografie; detaillierte bibliografische Daten sind im Internet über
<http://dnb.d-nb.de> abrufbar.

First English edition
© 2006 Psychosozial-Verlag
e-mail: info@psychosozial-verlag.de
www.psychosozial-verlag.de
Cover: © Ralf Vogt
Draft design cover: Atelier Warminski, Büdingen
Printed in Germany
ISBN 978-3-89806-700-3

Table of Contents

Note:

Since the German term "beseelen" or "beseelbar" can hardly be translated, it was left in the original. The word "Seele" has the meaning of *soul, mind, psyche*, and the verb "beseelen" would mean adding a soul, mind, psyche to an object. The term "beseelbare Therapieobjekte" has already been translated by "ensoulable therapy objects", but since this doesn't really capture the meaning, we left it in the original.

1 My Own Approach of Structural Activity-Specific Performances with Symbolizing Objects

Preliminary Notes

According to my previous therapeutic experience, orienting structures help to accelerate psychical healing processes and processes of change, and to make the necessary offers of relationship during a therapy more transparent and thereby also more effective.

In classical psychoanalysis, I feel, there is still a model prevailing to some extent that keeps patients at times too passive, ignorant and immature in the therapeutic setting; this, however, has never at all been the proclaimed aim of analytical work. Yet everything also has its effectsindependently from our intentions – as a sort of subliminal self-dynamics.

If the therapist is silent – without the patient understanding the *meaning and purpose as tested by himself or herself* or *approving* it in the specific human alliance –, such a wait-and-see passivity will from my point of view also entail a labilizing disorientation which, according to our classical doctrine, is to trigger an individual association process which in its contents shall then gradually shed light on the origin of the disorder (see Laplanche and Pontalis, 1991, p. 410 ff.).

But what if such a labilization does not trigger any important memories or creative ideas, nor uncover any connections, but instead possibly just re-evokes (retraumatizing) previous disquieting circumstances of life in a depressive patient? Or what if a more self-confident patient rejects this technique for just this reason? Why is it that precisely this passive wait-and-see way is supposed to be the most effective way to trigger psychoanalytic insights and changes? Why is it that the therapist's interpretations were viewed as the main way of classical psyochoanalytic work? Is the classical setting really the best form of working for the patient or is it rather the most distant and safest definition of the relationship for the therapist (see Pohlen and Bautz-Holzherr, 1995)?

I am not able to discuss these contradictory issues comprehensively in this book, yet I would consciously like to do my part to ensure that structural alternatives in psychotherapeutic work are made known and to promote a discourse among colleagues.

1.1 My Own Concept of a Mutual Relationship-Based Structure in a Psychotherapeutic Working Relationship

My own considerations regarding the mutual relationship-based structure of my psychotherapeutic work are based on early analytic experiences and writings of Sandor Ferenczi who lived from 1873 to 1933.

Modifications of this concept may also be found in the work of his disciple, Michael Balint (1936; 1970). During the last year of his life, Ferenczi undertook a psychoanalytic treatment experiment with a patient (see Fortune, 1994) which was recorded only in his private clinical diary of 1932 and which was first published only in 1985 – when a certain renaissance of his views emerged 50 years after his death (see Ermann, 1994, p. 707).

In the 1920s, Ferenczi developed the "active technique" (ibid.) which increasingly gave up the Freudian setting and his interpretation of the concept of abstinence in order to avoid that a patient having to re-experience any re-traumatizing experiences of failing parents (ibid, p. 709). Similar views have also been presented by contemporary analytic body-psychotherapists such as Moser (1987) or Heisterkamp (1993).

Ferenczi (1921, 1928, 1931, 1932 or 1964, 1988) tried at great cost to himself to find new ways that would make it easier for the client to recall his or her deprivations or any psychic damage suffered in childhood and to create a therapeutic substitute for them. Ermann (1944, p. 711) reproaches Ferenczi for at first wanting to enhance the client's recollection and re-activation of a trauma by means of the psychoanalytic technique and then later using the interpersonal attitude of the *substitute as a good object* to try to avoid such a re-activation of the trauma, at the same time, however, producing a therapeutically inappropriate attitude which in the end pre-programmed his failure.

That is not exactly how I see it. It is of course true that the neurotic structure of a repressed neediness may lead to the occurrence of regression-based obsessions and to indigestive destruction-oriented hatred in the patient during a therapeutically enhanced analysis process; but this had already been critically appreciated as a problem by Ferenczi himself during his time (see Ferenczi, 1928). For me the main difficulty of his therapy approach is that he wanted to solve the conflict "alone – for the patient". He had in fact recognized important interactional aspects of the psychoanalytic working relationship and was prepared to undertake risky experiments based on a self-opening. But obviously the deep appreciation of the patient's personality as well as the broad acceptance of and compassion for the clients' infantile deficits led him to the point where he failed to recognize the *parallelism of early and current personality structures.* The *adult* sides of the patient *can and must also* be brought *into co-operation* with the self-healing process. What is nested in this problem from my point of view is that the importance of the resistance sides against any process of change in the form of "acquired introjects" in the personality structure of the patient had been widely underestimated and is still being underestimated at times today. These parts, *along with the transference parts*, operate more or less permanently parallel, and thus sometimes suddenly change what is happening in the relationship (see section 4 below).

Apart from such difficulties, Ermann's (1994, s. 713-715) line of reasoning is, however, comprehensible to me when pointing out that biographic particularities – such as Ferenczi's ambivalent, unresolved relationship to his mother – were also responsible for the boundary difficulties Ferenczi experienced in connection with his patients. On the other hand, he also criticizes as too short Ferenczi's training analysis with Freud, during which precisely the reservoir of negative transferences was not dealt with sufficiently, a matter which Ferenczi *himself* had at that time already complained about Freud (see Ferenczi's letter to Freud of 1930 – quoted by Ermann, 1994, s. 174).

Had Ferenczi perhaps developed with his caring, empathetic procedure an approach that he might also have wished for himself from his supervising therapist?

Be that as it may, for me it is clear that Ferenczi's experimental culmination was a mutual analysis with "R.N." in which he strived on an equal footing for a shared regression and reciprocally exchanged the roles of analyst and analysand depending on where he thought the main cause of a blockade in the relationship was to be found just at that moment, in order to reach a next stage of deep acceptance (see Fortune, 1994, Ferenczi's diary of 1932 – published 1988). In the end, Ferenczi gave up his investigations of a mutual analysis, reproaching himself that he would not, after all, be sufficiently competent to be able to help the client with his closeness, etc. (see Ermann, 1994, p. 716).

Unfortunately, this one-sided admission was quickly used at that time as it is partially still used today – and perhaps even unconsciously gratefully used – to reject his experimental direction completely. At the congress in Wiesbaden in 1932, Ferenczi – as a former president of the International Psychoanalytic Association – was almost banned from speaking, standing virtually alone with his thoughts and feelings (Dupont, 1972 and 1985 – ibid.).

The concept of a nourishing replenishing of deficits in the psychoanalysis of basic disorders in patients was adopted by his disciple Balint (1936, 1970) and by other authors such as Winnicott (1974) and Bion (1971) – but the aspect of an active mutual relationship development has been ignored since then.

What I personally also find appealing in connection with the idea of a "reciprocally regressive relationship development to the mutual benefit of both", besides the high cooperative effectivity, is the later chance of an interpersonally most mature completion of a relationship that has grown over time. In my opinion, the quality of the mutual relationship could precisely be the successful ideal completion of a long-term analyticaltherapy. Here the aim of the relationship development need not necessarily be an exchange of roles but could rather be a mature experience of change taking place in a harmonious dissolution of the role differences between parents versus child or between healthy versus sick individuals. What would also be quite possible is that the "former" therapist and the "former" patient later have a shared socio-political concern.

The main difference to Ferenczi's approach is, however, that we as therapists in the first place clearly assume the leadership when establishing the relationship and in developing testable analysis qualities for the dissolution of transference and introject structures, as well as by requesting the patient to make his or her own cooperative, active contribution for entering into new relationship forms – as a voluntary option. As therapists, we thus proceed *only as indicated* in a mutual relationship-based way during the actual therapeutic activity-specific performance. From that point of view, the mutual approach in the development structure takes place in a controlled, shared interaction regression within a limited time for the overwhelming majority of the patients, where both the therapist and the patient always also retain their progressive self-control capacities. The mutual relationship-based regressive atmosphere is, however, if it can actually be reached, in its analytical effectivity far superior to a one-sided regression offer (or worse: a one-sided regression request).

A major problem of the classical psychoanalytical setting is from my point of view, as mentioned before, that too many therapeutic explanation and orientation structures are withheld from the patient, with the consequence and tendency that the patient is underestimated in the progressive relationship development.

My style of working in the opening phase of the relationship in a universal psychotherapy with structural activity-specific performances, where a certain number of the hours of work has to be determined at the beginning of the therapy, has changed in the meantime in that I proceed psycho-educationally at the beginning of the therapy, i.e. after having explored the patient's pathology, I take the time to explain to him or her calmly the terms of transference, countertransference, introject, defense dynamics, regression, role structures of various inner personality traits, re-performance of relationship disturbance experiences and others, in order a) not to produce any unproductive labilization *due to ignorance or unawareness and due to the fact that information has been withheld*, and b) to filter out simpler cases requiring consultation in the run-up to the actual psychotherapy.

The mutual quality of a relationship begins with a *well-informed patient* who is better able to cope with the structure of the setting and who will thus be in a position to take a joint decision for changing the setting. Only then can a patient assume, and is willing to assume for himself or herself, responsibility for the therapeutic success. In addition, the mutual relationship-based procedure within the patient-therapist-relationship implies that the therapist also engages himself or herself in an (according to my understanding) active, regressive interaction milieu in the movement with the patient, while, however, always keeping in mind the meaning and purpose of this joint initiative, commenting and modifying it, if necessary, so that the aim of the agreed therapeutic structure can be reached. If it is important for reducing a negative relationship transference, the therapist will also accept certain interaction wishes of the patient (e.g. for anxiety reduction, creating something together or developing dialogues with stuffed animals or further similar interactions, see also below section 2.), in order to immerse himself or herself in the regression in a way which will be *experienceable for the patient* – or sometimes also to be ahead of the patient in an exemplary way.

This is basically a behaviour which is also practiced by parents when dealing with their children, for example when they learn to swim, in order to reduce the child's anxiety. Here it would also be unpedagogical and heartless to just throw a child into the water and to say: "I also had to learn it this way, so make an effort!" The mutual relationship-based approach is perhaps also an approach that works on a more partnership-oriented basis and with a more positive change of transference than it would be possible with a merely observing, physically inactive attitude. The reduction of the therapy time and the sustainability of the successfully changed relationship is a good result of such a mutual approach (see also case examples under 2.).

What is basically difficult for the therapist is only that he or she has to bear a certain (new) feeling of insecurity that is brought about by leaving the familiar setting, and that he or she has to gain in advance the necessary self-experience for such a work. In connection with these shared competences, the aim must also be to elaborate the necessary criteria in respect to the case example, i.e. to determine if a mutual relationship-based approach has been *sufficiently well prepared* and whether or not it could serve the current change of transference or a new experimental exploration of the patient's development. Mutual relationship-based interaction offers should not be applied if the therapist is bothered by inner anxieties that this might be an excessive demand for him or her, if the therapist fears certain introject or transference sides of the patient where the therapist is not at all able to work on them verbally satisfactorily, or if the therapist gives in to the patient's pressure or to the helper's role simply out of an obscure uncertainty.

In some "lucky cases", a regressive atmosphere could also emerge here – it has not, however, been defined in a structural-therapeutical sense so that it cannot be *effectively evaluated*. This requires a certain relationship-based dynamic level in the therapy where as a matter of principle all important basic emotions – such as anger, grief, anxiety, love, emptiness, etc. – have occured at least once and have been perceived as such between the two individuals, and could be addressed well – i.e. worked on well –, because no reliable working alliance would otherwise be possible for an experimental mutual relationship and an extension of the mutual relationship, or would not be therapeutically justifiable.

During analytical supervisions, colleagues kept asking me whether or not the "whole psychoanalytical effect would not fizzle out", if and when transferences were addressed so early and the therapeutical-methodical context was explained so frankly. I definitely think this is not so.

And if a transference could be dissolved so easily, then this would rather indicate an educational deficit on the part of the patient which need not be treated with any extravagant dynamic performances but should be sufficiently solvable by a simple, friendly explanation.

Yet, real and serious transferences as they are brought about by neurotic developments still occur in manifold ways also after vivid explanations are given, and they can be treated better and all in all within a shorter period of time with the patient's *identified cooperation*, if *these structures are also well-understandable and transparent for the patient*, because he or she partially gets the respective know-how to initiate, control, and evaluate them for himself or herself.

What is needed in the therapeutic working alliance to make sure that a mutual relationship-based relationship can be developed between the patient and the therapist in the future is at present in the first place an adult EGO and an intellectual-emotional, somewhat distant EGO that is capable of working and that can voluntarily and seriously assume the responsibility for the shared process consciously.

This includes also the client's readiness to consciously venture to the *negative transference sides of the working relationship* and once they have been uncovered to also take here and now *small initiatives for reducing them*. The therapist may also be given small tasks in this context which he can then in turn realize voluntarily and to the conscious benefit of both within in the framework of his capacity for self-experience, in order to reduce his share in any "superfluous" transference. The procedure may be demonstrated best in detail by an example, as described in connection with the case of treatment of Sven Reimann under 2.1.1. and 2.1.2. (see below).

In the course of the therapy, the currently experienced relationship will be perceived, discussed and changed in *increasingly similar fashion between the patient and the therapist*. Due to the mutual completion of the treatment relationship, the therapist can in the end also be discharged to return to his or her "normal life", thus enhancing the human detachment the most natural way.

1.2 Major Elements of Therapeutic Reciprocity

Psychic problems exist in the experience and behavior of individuals in connection with themselves and towards other people. Usually, they are brought about in the course of the development of life due to the influence of close and/or responsible reference persons or attachment figures, stored in the individual's memory, and determine today his or her functioning in society as well as his or her goal orientations.

A structural and universal therapy approach should address and deal with in a proven association adequate solution patterns based on *interactional disorder analyses and change-specific orientations*. The reciprocally complicated experience systems, that also occur during *the joint work* between the patient and the therapist *here and now* are particularly taken into consideration here. The old disorder patterns are reproduced again in the experimental interaction behavior and reflected together, in order to try out ideas for possible solutions.

Otherwise the therapist who wants to help a patient to get out of a depressive crisis could, for example, quickly run into the danger of overforming the individual seeking advice with his own ideas regarding the development, or of manifesting old dependency structures so that they become chronic, or of being crushed by rigid introjects of the client, coupled with "never-ending relapses", or of getting worn and torn as a result of his or her helper's syndrome.

The client's own therapeutic competence which is to be built up and has to be developed with the patient and fortified in the first place is from my point of view to be considered as the only way out of the permanent dialectics of "wanting help" and of "preventing therapy" in the patient.

The patient's self-perception of his personality, his capability of interpreting his own behavior, as well as his own analyses of problems and his activities aiming at developing a solution also imply that we as therapists have to share our therapeutical basic knowledge, our doubts, and our solution-oriented expectations *in an orderly way and step by step* so that it can be used for an increasingly more independent self-treatment by the patient.

The difficulty in this connection is that the client's capabilities and competences in respect to an analysis of the symptoms, of working on resistances, and of testing behavior have to be developed and trained to that end in the first place, so that his *own work* will neither do any harm to himself nor to others but rather helps to develop a healthy potential for change.

Some important principles governing such a structural-universal approach are from my point of view the following:

1) The therapeutic work should be marked by a high degree of current descriptiveness in diagnostic and therapeutical respects. That means, for example, that a verbal depiction of the symptoms will not be sufficient, but that the therapist will have to look for ways to generate the problem here and now in a controlled way and to work on it in an exemplary way by different experimental sequences of behavior.

2) Together with the client, transparent therapy structures are developed, substantiated, agreed upon, and verified on the basis of the results.

3) The therapeutic cooperation requires from both sides a high degree of motivation concerning the relationship, the shared claim to understand or to uncover the background of a disorder, and to work on it within the framework of current solution-oriented possibilities on the basis of reconciled mutual activities (mutual relationship and treatment objective).

4) The therapeutic work takes account, to a high degree, of the dialectically necessary reciprocity of regression and progression, subject and object, as well as of the introject and transference. With regard to the regression and progression aspects, the capability of emotional tuning is to be trained, and adult switching and transfer competencies are to be developed and extended. This includes, for example, also an extension of the patient's emotional structure, to be able to distance himself or herself from the experience for a short time, and the courage to dar infantile or archaic spontaneity for defined experiments.

The subject-object aspect means, from my point of view, first that the patient can see himself or herself in the interaction reciprocally both as the reacting and the performing part of the relationship. Second, certain symbolizing objects are to be used in the therapy to perceive psychic structures in the subjective meaning-related atmosphere and to explore individual trial actions aiming at a solution of the symptoms by means of these objects.

Third, the subject-object-aspect also refers to the dynamic connection between the individual and the group. It is strived for as a treatment criteria within the therapeutic work in the form of a changing setting, so that, for example, the results gained through the individual therapy can be verified and extended in a group setting as a possible mirror of the environment and vice versa. Due to the self-help nature of its structure, the group is also a field of social experimentation for confrontation, education, and solidarity.

The aspect of reciprocity between introject and transference is explicitly emphasized in this approach, because it refers to one of the most important conceptual innovations.

In my opinion, a transference does not exist without a corresponding introject pertaining to it which *helps to "secure" the dynamic manifestation of the pathology so that it becomes chronic* – so to speak, as an alleged product of the previous relationship experience in the patient's disturbed development system.

That means that if therapeutic efforts are made to reduce the client's transference, the resistance of the introject has to be reckoned with and has also be included in the therapy. This will again give rise to a transference resistance, etc. In the therapeutic working process, it is always the most obvious accents that have to be dealt with.

In order to reduce the "dynamic wear" in this psychotherapeutic work to a minimum, the therapeutic work focuses, as a matter of principle – according to the above-mentioned conceptual premises – more *on working on the transference than in the transference.* The same applies to the therapeutic work *on the introject – rather than against the introjects*, so that less destructive psychodynamic is provoked – and hence less a danger of retraumatization.

1.3 My Own Approach of the Use of Objects, Transference, and Role Play Performances

1.3.1 The Approach of Transitional Transference Objects

The concept of transitional transference objects has already been described in a number of publications in the last three years (see Vogt, 2001 a-e; 2002 a-c, 2003).

For this reason, interested readers are asked to please refer to these publications for more details, and only a very brief extract of the approach will be presented here. For me, an important objective of my psychotherapeutic work with clients is to transform the patient's serious background conflicts to some extent – including working on and changing these conflicts – into vividly manageable scene images or pictures. The aim is to make the diagnostics of disorder patterns *more easily comprehensible for the patient* and to make *the symptom complexes, with playful earnestness, experimentally* solvable at certain points for the patient here and now, *based on the therapy to be derived from the diagnostics.*

Furthermore, we know from trauma research (see Huber, 2003 a, b; van der Kolk et al., 2000) that affectively strongly charged experiences are only *fragmentarily stored* and can therefore only be made conscious and worked on in therapy when *the traumatizing scene is actively approached.* The disadvantage of a classical analytical couch setting is also that symptom-specific atmospheres cannot be "touched" or "provoked" with such a monotonous lying position, which cannot really be associated by the patient, despite all his or her will or any momentary resistance, without experiencing a *currently triggered influence.*

In the course of the last seven years, I have in an empirical-experimental effort *consciously produced symbolizing objects* which correspond in a mixture of a *playful and earnest form* to the recounted conflict-ridden, stressful, and sometimes traumatizing situations – as they were described to me by many advanced patients.

The aim was to build objects or to use existing objects that are able to help the client within a relatively short time to atmospherically return to and to immerse himself or herself in parts of the original stressful situation, in spite of any massive fears of contact. With regard to the relationship, efforts are made here to relieve the often deadlocked negative transference situations by disassembling them to a triangulating partial object, since the therapist would ultimately like to work calmly and precisely with the patient *on the problem of the unconscious transference.* Furthermore, these intermediate objects often also help to defuse the frequently described danger of sexualization in analytical body-psychotherapy due to the real distance created by the objects and the *observable* impressive regressive atmosphere.

Since the supplementary therapy object *transitionally* thus assumes a difficult *transference part*, I use the term of a "transitional transference object" to refer to it in structural universal psychotherapy.

Besides certain similarities to Winnicott's term of transitional objects (Winnicott, 1953 – quoted in Petzold and Sieper, 1996) and Petzold's term of intermediary objects (see Petzold, 1996; Vogt, 2002 c), this definition also contains some differentiating points.

One important difference is that the transitional transference objects of adult clients are *consciously "beseelt"*, in order to represent a side of the transference of the former and now repeatedly experienced emotional experience in the relationship structure. That means that *after the client's progressive return* from the therapy setting, they will *no longer constantly* affect the relationship to the therapist as atmospheric regressive objects (see also below 1.3.1.1). Contrary to the transitional objects of a child, they do not have primarily any *supporting function* but rather an interaction-enhancing function. And thirdly, they are *not a substitute symbol* for any person, but more an *atmospheric feature* of the psychic problem-specific experience of the patient.

By using transitional transference objects the therapist is in a position to shift from the strongly affectively-charged work *in the transference* – to the emotionally often more effective relationship type – to work *on the transference*, in particular, because the clarifying interaction-related work can be more easily and more vividly differentiated this way (see also below 1.3.2).

Below you will find three graphs illustrating how a therapist might change by means of an intermediate transitional transference object from his or her verbal work *in the transference* to an activity-oriented joint work *on the transference*.

Graph 1: This breakdown of the transference often serves the purpose of discharging the transference.

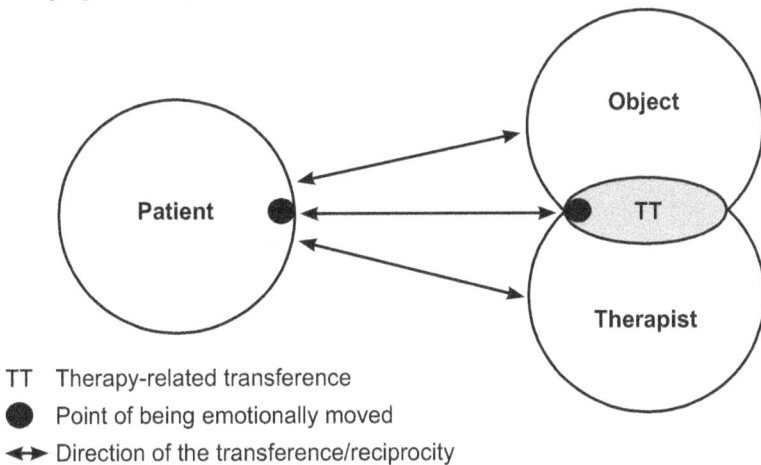

TT   Therapy-related transference
●   Point of being emotionally moved
◄► Direction of the transference/reciprocity

Graph 2: This organization of the transference often serves the purpose of exploring the transference.

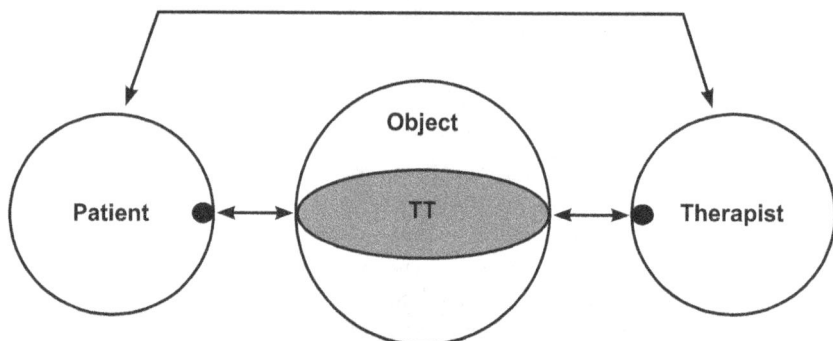

TT   Therapy-related transference
●   Point of being emotionally moved
◄►   Direction of the transference/reciprocity

Graph 3: The transference setting often serves the purpose of opening the transference

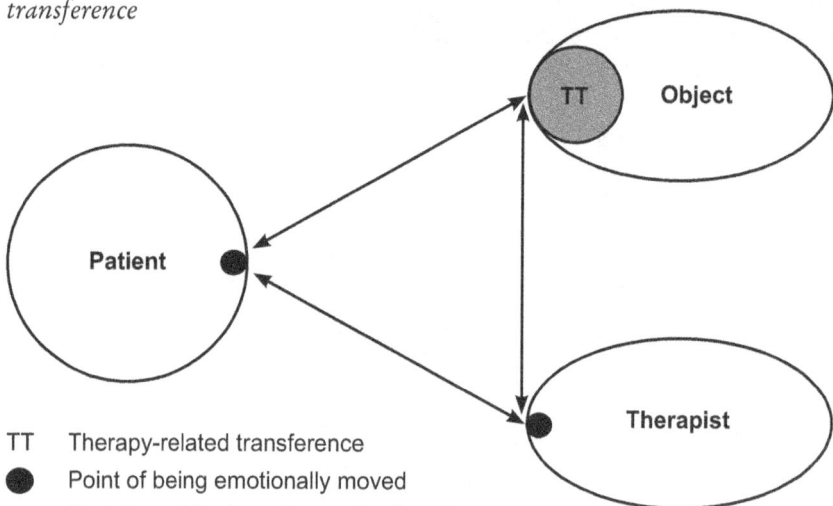

TT   Therapy-related transference
●   Point of being emotionally moved
◄►   Direction of the transference/reciprocity

The momentary relationship-specific atmosphere between the patient and the therapist, as well as the spontaneous level of the "psychic trigger" of the impression-specific, vaguely associatively and emotionally laden objects ("Anmutungsobjekte") according to the special individual psychic back-

ground of the client's experience decide how playful or earnest the transference-related atmosphere will be. But also in respect to the countertransference of the therapist, there will be new chances and spontaneous possibilities
of invention for psychotherapeutic interaction-related work.

This way, the therapist can *bear* far more negative transference offers in
the patient's active activity-related offensive (*Graph 1*) *or also respond to
them (Graph 2)*, which would hardly be feasible *with merely verbal reaction possibilities* or personal physical movements and gestures. Furthermore,
by using the intermediate objects in the contact with the patient, forms of
touching will be possible in the interaction (with a client who is quite capable
of work immediately) that would in the case of a direct skin-to-skin contact
sometimes only be realizable after 50 therapy sessions.

The aim of using transitional transference objects is hence not the use as
such but the *early or graduated immediate interaction* between client and
therapist (Graph 2). This possibility will usually also help to reduce any unproductive countertransference attitudes on the part of the therapist, because
he or she can also be relieved on a therapy-indicated basis by the direct activity-related offers and is not forced to stick to any one-sided observation
attitudes (perhaps like a non-helping parent). Otherwise he or she might possibly even still generate any additional negative transference energy which
would ultimately counteract his or her "task to differentiate" as a therapist.
On the other hand, the therapist's chances of movement should not enhance
any premature, non-indicated, and non-structured actions, but rather actively advance a dosed joint dissolution of the blockades – to the benefit of both
sides – here and now.

As illustrated in Graph 3, the therapist will better be able to elucidate the
structure of the disturbed psychic activiation of a symptom for the client, if
the client realizes, due to the encouraging help of a transitional transference
object, that he *changes his psychic states under his vaguely associatively and
emotionally laden impression ("Anmutung") of the object* and that, while he
is *actively involved in an activity-related performance with an object*, completely forgotten or "other" ideas out of his past come to his mind which are
promoted with object performances by the therapist.

Because the therapist also has his or her own parallel experiences during
the small interaction experiments with the objects where, in order to be able
to work empathetically and spontaneously, he or she cannot slip into any ra-
tionale permanent observation for too long, the therapist will no longer perceive the client in the countertransference as so "incurable and chronically
rigid in his attitudes". *The therapist will feel the insecurities of the interaction
himself or herself too*, by which a mutual relationship-based working atmo-

sphere will be enhanced. During a joint aggression-related exercise, within the framework of the therapy, it will then also be permissble for the therapist to release his or her frustration – to an appropriate degree, as demonstrated by the patient. This reduces his or her countertransference, increases his or her credibility, and helps to improve his or her empathy within a few minutes. Ultimately, this procedure of an indicated reduction of the counter-transference even serves the preservation or restoration of the therapeutic psycho-hygiene, what will, of course, pay off for both the patient and the therapist in long-term treatments.

1.3.1.1 Construction and Representation of the Transitional Transference Objects

The "beseelte 'character'" of the transitional transference objects results from two aspects:

a) from the potential regressive-archaic power of the subliminal vaguely associatively and emotionally laden impression of the object, and
b) from the realized "beseelten" use of the object within the specific interaction between the patient and the therapist.

In order to be able to create the power of the vaguely associatively and emotionally laden impression in the form of an object, the empirical method of patient interviews was selected. The point was to find out which *psychic atmosphere a patient refers to*, when he or she feels his psychic problem as a problem, e.g.: "That is as barely comprehensible, as stressful, as intangible ... – as with the mother, father, clique, the working group", etc. (see construction principles, Vogt, 2001 a, b).

Thereafter, I built objects according to the trial-and-error principle and then verified with these patients whether or not these objects "let them feel the same or something similar", whether or not the feeling could be more vividly or clearer understood by "comprehending (touching)" the object, or the like.

Below follows a reference to earlier publications (Vogt, ibid.) and a selection of the transitional transference objects most often used, by presenting photographs coupled with the most frequent empirical criteria for use. Even though I decided to present the objects by means of photographs, I would like to point out to the reader that the vaguely associatively and emotionally laden impression of the object can only be partially conveyed this way, because you must *directly see and feel the large bodies in front of you* in order to be able to enter into the psychic oscillation; for this reason, I indicated the measurements as a sort of supplement to your imagination. Large objects tend to bring about more readily an alienation between the space and a "peculiar world of danger" through which a *regressive effect* can be triggered, enabling the therapist to work *on the transference*.

This self-dynamic effect of the transitional transference objects differs, so that I distinguish roughly between objects where factor A (see above) – the implicitly vaguely associatively and emotionally laden impression – is predominant or where factor B (see above) – the "beseelte" use – tends to plays a more important part. The degree of use procides the opportunity, particularly in the establishment of alternative interaction and selection structure for the patient, through which the milieu of the transference can be well explored. Here I will confine myself on this topic to just a few keynotes and would ask you to please refer to the sections with the case examples for more details, as any further explanations would exceed the scope of this book.

The photographs referring to this text may be found in the appendex under 4.1. (see appendix).

Color, weight, material, and contents are empirically tested and well-founded, and thus also copyrighted for my own security and protection against any inappropriate use, as well as for the protection of the small sales company and its subcontractors.

I. The Red Giant Block
Measurements in cm: 150x80x80 (smaller ones: 80x80x60; 60x60x45)

Ambiguous statements of patients *regarding the vaguely associatively and emotionally laden impression*:
- "It makes me furious."
- "It is more powerful than all others."
  "It doesn't permit anything."
- "I want to topple it over."
- "I want to sit on it." And so on.

Frequent use in therapy:
- in role play constellations and role play statements, symbolization of the strict, feared, violent family member;
- in individual and group therapy, target object for releasing aggression by means of a club or kicks;
- power-pushing of the patient against the therapist
- pedestal, altar, rock for various performances of the client, and many more.

23

II. The Giant Limp Bag

Measurements in cm: Ø 140x70 (medium size: Ø 95x45; smaller one: Ø 65x40)

Ambiguous statements of patients *regarding the vaguely associatively and emotionally laden impression*:
- "I would like to pound on it."
- "I can't get hold of it."
- "When kicking into it, I get feelings of helplessness."
- "When looking at it longer, I get the feeling of being lonesome and sad."
- "I would like to lie on it – like in a nest." And more of the same.

Frequent use in therapy:
- in role play constellations and role play statements of the patient, symbolization of the indulgent, unbearably weak or dead family member;
- in individual and group therapy, target object of murderous anger expressed with a club or with kicks;
- experiencing helplessness when grasping into it in an empty, weak manner;
- experiencing load by carrying it around and by lying under it;
- nest, rock, repulsive person, dunghill, among other things, for various performances of the patient, and the like.

III. The White Wall

Measurements in cm: 250x120x20

Ambiguous statements of patients *regarding the vaguely associatively and emotionally laden impression*:
- "You're powerless against it."
- "That is like a struggle in fog against a superior power."
- "It has an effect like a slammed door."
- "I want to pull this wall down."
- "I must kick against it." And more of the same.

Frequent use in therapy:
- in role play constellations and role play statement, symbol for a great nebulous power in the family;
- in individual therapy, target object for releasing aggression by means of a club, by throwing the bag, or by kicks;
- running against a wall in life;

- icy wall, emptiness, closed door, unassailable power or similar performances.

IV. The Giant Mat
Measurements in cm: 250x230x22

Ambiguous statements of patients *regarding the vaguely associatively and emotionally laden impression*:
- "Well, that's like a big meadow for romping."
- "That has the effect of a never-ending area in the nowhere."
- "It makes you feel so tiny."
- "It is really like a giant ice floe on the sea."
- "Here you can lash out and scream like mad." And the like.

Frequent use in therapy:
- in individual and group therapy, as a play area;
- in individual therapy, as a baby's bed;
- in individual therapy, as a mat for beating and holding in connection with grief-related subjects in a lying position; "association-earth-couch", and much more of the same.

V. The Giant Tub
Measurements in cm: height 150 cm x outside Ø 80; inside Ø 54; *load:* approx. 150 kgs; *weight:* approx. 50 kgs

Ambiguous statements of patients *regarding the vaguely associatively and emotionally laden impression*:
- "Here I get claustrophobia."
- "I could lie and stay in here for ever."
- "Now I would like to keep rolling around endlessly in the tub's belly."
- "You can't hug it so well, although I would like to."
- "I am feeling depressed and abandoned." (sitting in it)

Frequent use in therapy:
- in individual therapy, for releasing phobic symptoms;
- in individual and group therapy, roles in games, or in connection with role play performances symbol for a smooth, difficult person you can't take hold of or for a powerful, flattening person (roller);
- in individual therapy, the child's small sickbed or tub for hiding;
- sitting near the upright standing tub and in the hole when feeling depres-

sively lost;
- a person's standoffish hugging or a baby's birth canal, and many more of the same.

VI. The Giant Egg

Measurements in cm: outside diameter approx. 150; inside diameter approx. 120, room for approx. two adults or three children

Ambiguous statements of patients *regarding the vaguely associatively and emotionally laden impression*:
- "It scares me that it is like a snapping mouth."
- "I feel so safe and sheltered in there like in a womb."
- "In this hiding-place I can tell my bad story."
- "I would like to roll around with it on the spot."
- "That is a protected world that I never had."

Frequent use in therapy:
- in individual therapy, for releasing phobic symptoms;
- Working on birth-related subjects or a special birth trauma;
- exploration of particularly shame-bound subjects;
- provision of a specific shelter for a child;
- play booth, nest, cave for rolling around, world for cuddling, and the like;
- performances of individual and group therapy as a special mystery ball, and much more of the same.

VII. The Hover Belt

Measurements in cm: length 200 cm, fastening loops every 12 cm

Ambiguous statements of patients *regarding the vaguely associatively and emotionally laden impression*:
- "I feel carried like a baby."
- "The hovering above the ground scares me."
- "The slight swinging makes me absolutely sad – the faces look so big."
- "It makes me so sad that there are so many who are taking care of me."

Frequent use in therapy:
- hovering and holding exercises in group therapy;
- stretcher in the group;
- baby cradle – baby swing in the group, and many more of the same.

VIII. The Harnesses
Measurements: Available as children's or adults' harness

Ambiguous statements of patients *regarding the vaguely associatively and emotionally laden impression*:
- "In here I immediately feel held again like in a baby's playpen."
- "I get the feeling I am strong as a horse."
- "I get massive feelings of helplessness, if I an not making any headway."
- "If I feel this belt in my back, I can go to my limits better."

Frequent use in therapy:
- baby's belt scenes, horse games in the group;
- simulation of helplessness with holding parents or living conditions;
- tether in connection with a major release of aggression;
- development of aggressive dialogues between two arguing partners.

IX. The Clubs
Measurements: Available as children's or adults' clubs

Ambiguous statements of patients *regarding the vaguely associatively and emotionally laden impression*:
- "With the club I am double as strong as otherwise."
- "With the club I feel my anger more clearly."
- "Finally, I can bang without any consideration."

Frequent use in therapy:
- release of aggression on bags or blocks and the like;
- mobilization of archaic powers in patients with weaknesses in establishing boundaries;
- release of frustration for hyperactive children and adults, and many similar uses.

X. The Rope
Measurements: 4 m; $\varnothing$ 2 cm (larger one: 6 m; $\varnothing$ 4 cm, or group rope: 10 m; $\varnothing$ 4,5 cm)

Ambiguous statements of patients *regarding the vaguely associatively and emotionally laden impression*:
- "With this, I really feel your support throughout my body."
- "The rope encourges me to plunge even deeper into my inner self."

- "The rope appears to me like an extended hand."
- "I experience the rope like an umbilical cord – out of the egg / out of the belly."

Frequent use in therapy:
- liana swing for children or childlike adults;
- holding rocker between patent and therapist;
- group's tugging rope for up to 12 persons;
- "accompanying hand" in connection with difficult anxiety-related and helplessness-relating subjects on the mat, in the tub or in the egg;
- umbilical cord symbol in connection with birth-related subjects.

XI. Additional Symbols as Transitional Transference Objects

Apart from those mentioned above, there are additional objects that are used for body-therapeutic-symbolizing applications. They are associated with some similar transitional transference-related vaguely associatively and emotionally laden impressions or with less ambiguous expressiveness.

They are, however, often effective performance aids when used in the patient's "beseelte" experience. Due to space constraints, they are described below in just one sentence:

1) *Hammock.* The hammock has an effect similar to the hover belt and somewhat in the direction of the giant tub and the egg. It is especially useful as a baby cradle or a child's bed in individual therapy.
2) *Swing.* The swing leads back to the age of an infant and school-child (lower grade), thus enhancing regression. It is suitable as a comfortable object for "incidental talks" (good parents/grandparents relationship).
3) *Swinging bag.* Used in a deeper regression as a swinging pear-like shaped bag or for hanging on to a "beseelten" body (cling to, and the like). In other contexts also used as a punching or boxing bag for aggressions.
4) *Yellow bag.* Used as a punching bag for pushing or throwing (hit each other's arguments over the head with the therapist or with fellow patients, etc.). But sometimes also a body symbol of one's own for the inner child (suitable for holding on to).
5) *Belly pillow.* Primarily has the function of clinging to it or of giving support in case of states of anxiety in children and adults. Protects the belly in a lying position.
6) *Covers.* Provide protection and boundaries for children and adults; have the effect of caring hugs and hands in connection with regressions.
7) *Contact sticks.* Establish a contact also in cases of fears of contact. Provide

the possibility of subtle swinging exercises with finely differentiated instructions.

8) *Fingerball.* Suitable for contact plays and regressions in children's age (when playing on knees). The finger-contact-ball offers an excellent opportunity for subtle and spontaneous finger-and-hand-contacts between patient and therapist (infant – parents/grandparents and the like).

9) *Stuffed animals.* On the one hand, stuffed animals are suitable for family constellations or introject transference role plays (see below). On the other hand, stuffed animals are useful to establish a verbal contact on an infant-appropriate basis, or patients can be led into anxiety-related situations with the help of substitute dialogues (protector, observer, helper animals). When using stuffed animals it is important that a strongly expressive range of cuddly, ambiguous, and frightening animals is available.

I refrain from listing any further therapy objects, because we should confine ourselves for the moment primarily to the empirically researched symbolizing objects mentioned above.

1.3.1.2 The Special Problem of "Beseelen" and of the Indication for the Use of Objects

„Beseelen" and the indication of the therapy objects used are the core of the approach of transitional transference objects, because the structural frame of an adequate use of the therapy objects would otherwise get lost.

Symbolizing objects have been used in manifold ways in psychotherapy for a long time. During my family therapy training, I personally experienced them as extremely important in the playful encounter with children.

In concentrative movement therapy (see Becker, 1997) they are also common practice in adult psychotherapy. Gestalt therapists, bioenergetic therapists, and other professional colleagues use therapy materials on a routine basis.

According to Petzold and Sieper (1993), the use of symbolic materials and objects has been known in modern psychiatry since Reil (1803, quoted ibid.) and Janet (1925).

When attending and observing therapy sessions of concentrative movement therapists, bioenergetic therapists and other colleagues, I unfortunately found that often, the objects were not selected with therapeutically due care together with the patients or on the basis of a substantiated indication on the part of the therapist. Another shortcoming was that the perceptions of such objects on the part of the patient were not adequately explored, and that the patient's experience-related impetuses for action were not systematically followed up (which would at least be necessary afterwards following a spontaneous sequence of actions, with a certain distancing ability on the part of both parties!).

Ultimately, that means that the relationship to the therapist, the particularity of the current treatment phase, as well as the patient's specific symptom pattern were not always adequately considered when selecting the said therapy objects.

Secondly, in the above-mentioned therapy settings, the therapists unfortunately did without letting the specific patient feel a "beseelte" quality or describe it verbally in such a way that it would have gone beyond the purely technical property of the object (e.g. "That is a heavy material and a huge piece" versus "That is really hard and inconquerable as it is with my father").

Thirdly, what I also missed when I attended and observed these therapy sessions was that any visible emotional consternation in connection with the perception of the object used and the exemplarily triggered impetuses of action on the part of the patient, as well as the *trilogical reciprocity* between patient, object and therapist were consciously filtered out and followed up.

Of course, the above criticism does not mean that the use of the objects would have been generally wrong or therapeutically ineffective in this case. It does, however, mean that there may even be great analytical reserves with regard to the use of therapy objects, i.e. how their use can be more purposefully and ultimately thus also more effectively organized, or how therapeutic boomerang effects of any unsuccessful use of objects can find an important basis of explanation, so that the objects used are not merely *aids and tools of the therapist*, but can become "beseelte" *self-experience objects of the patient* (see Vogt, 2003).

In the above section 1.3.1.1, I described that some of the objects used already possess a power of „Beseelung", if they trigger a quality of a vaguely associatively and emotionally laden impression of a "special kind" in the patient (see above).

I would now like to define systematically the three different components of "Beseelen" of these objects as well as of more neutral objects as follows:

1) *"Beseelbare"* therapy objects are created as a result of the *conscious intention* of the therapeutic offer according to which the therapist wants to use symbolizing objects focus-orientationally in order to represent innerpsychic processes externally. The patient is consciously encouraged to look for a material expression of his or her inner emotional state as an image or a partial image of the feeling, character, conflict, etc. pertaining to it.

2) *"Beseelte"* objects are created within this search and adoption process as a result of the *specifically reflected emotional perception of the patient,* either because he or she accepts and engages in the quality of the vaguely associatively and emotionally laden impression of a therapy object to the extent that he or she feels the inner oscillation resonance in respect of a relevant subjective issue, or because he or she looks for an object giving the issue he or she focuses on a specific shape (e.g. by a comparison of objects), or because he or she builts up an atmospheric performance by means of the objects (e.g. by building a castle by means of the objects).

3) Symbolizing objects will be "beseelbar", if, after the selection of the objects, *a patient-specific experience and action-activating effect is achieved* that provides the possibility of self-diagnostic evidence and of self-created problem-solution structures on the part of the patient. Thereby a transitional change in the therapeutic transference situation will be brought about. In this context, "Beseelbarkeit" implies also that the "particular quality" of the object can be withdrawn or adequately reduced again after the end of the therapy session. That means that the therapeutically "beseelte" transitional transference character is not already brought about by the "mere existence" of an object, but only as a result of the *full modulation capacity.*

For more details regarding the terms of symbol and symbolization, please refer to Vogt (2003).

The indication for the use of therapy objects follows in the first place from the subtle relationship-based transference analysis between patient and therapist. If there are any *difficult changeable dissolution blockades* shaping the relationship, in spite of the fact that the *transference structures* have been perceived and *discussed,* or if a *further exploration of the transference areas* could be of any diagnostic benefit, the use of transitional transference objects should be considered. Of course, the basic terms and meanings of the specific transference structures must be known to the patient *beforehand.* Likewise, *any and all important qualities of an emotion such as anger, grief, helplessness, anxiety, emptiness, etc.* should already have occurred at least once in the relationship between the patient and the therapist and should already have been recognized and allocated to the patient as a transference and and to the therapist as a countertransference at least once in mutual agreement.

If the therapist, for example, still experiences strong fear, envy or helplessness in respect to the patient, he or she will not be able to reduce such deficiencies adequately well by adding any therapy objects, because the non-differentiated patient will "mess up" at the lastest the joint evaluation of the action-related scene, because the patient's resistance forces him or her to a permanent relationship disturbance, and because he or she experiences any offers to change the setting as just "another trick". Yet also with a more advanced patient, gross indication errors may occur, as the following graphic representations will show (see Vogt in Trautmann-Voigt, 2002).

Case A:
The therapist performs "what he or she thinks is right" – without the patient identifying with it. The therapist acts out his or her own problem in manipulation actions.
    The patient is belittled; the therapist stages himself or herself in the end.

Graph 4:

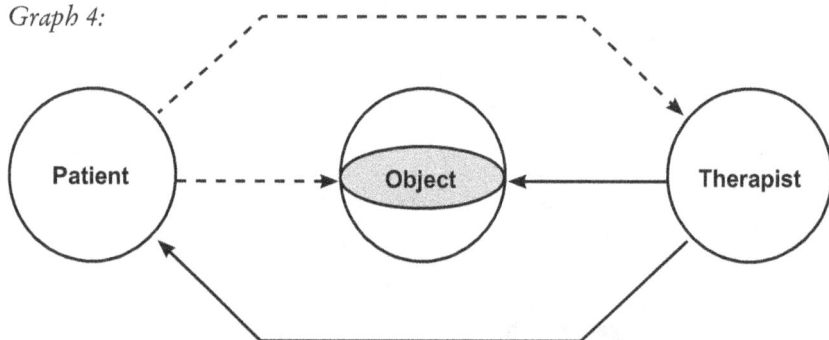

○ Possible potential power of the transference of the object
→ effective direction of the relationship (transference power)
--→ ineffective direction of the relationship (transference power)

Example:
The therapist "prescribes" the patient to punch as forcefully as possible on a bag because of his or her aggression inhibitions. The patient, however, does not identify himself or herself with it and experiences the therapist's request as an exposure or as nonsense.

Case B:
Therapist and patient perform something without any serious (regressive "beseelte") emotional involvement. The relevance of the therapy remains unclear; both are happy while acting, because they can perform unconscious substitute actions without any "dissolution pressure" (object I). Another important therapeutic object relationship (object II) remains unconsciously excluded.

Graph 5:

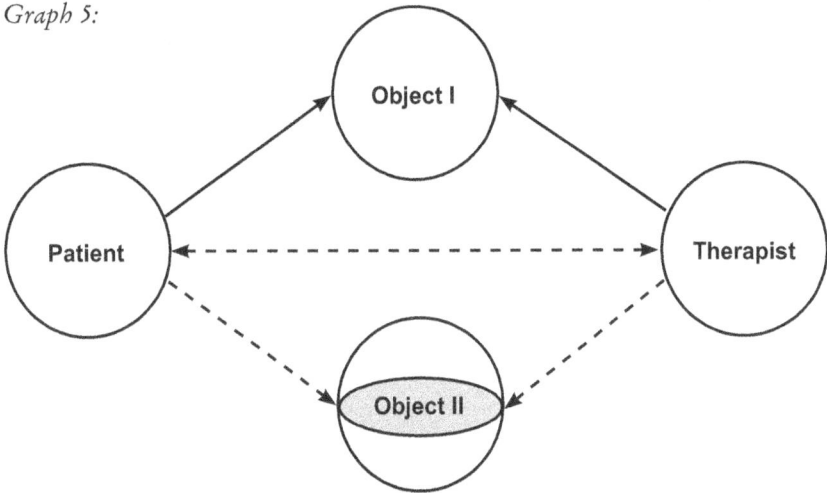

○ Possible potential power of the transference of the object
→ effective direction of the relationship (transference power)
--→ ineffective direction of the relationship (transference power)

Example:
The therapist or the patient gets the idea to work in the session today on a "father subject", and the patient then proceeds to punch on a big block to the point of a "satisfactory exhaustion". What remained unrecognized here was, that in his real life, the patient has a lot of trouble with his second divorce, because a latent abandonment on the part of the mother was not worked on. So, both acting partners are blocking out an important (but presumably threatening) subject with an "emotional misperformance.

Case C:
The patient performs his or her acting out of the problems without any therapeutic working alliance. The therapist is afraid of or "forgets" the clarification of the relationship and is so to say a victim of the patient's action-related power.

Graph 6:

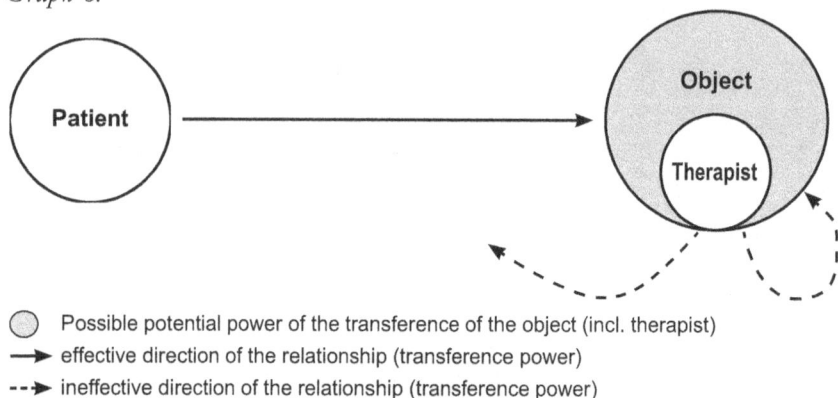

◯ Possible potential power of the transference of the object (incl. therapist)
→ effective direction of the relationship (transference power)
- -► ineffective direction of the relationship (transference power)

Example:
A physically very strong patient analyzes with his (slender) female therapist that he would finally have to establish a boundary in respect to his authoritative father. The therapist "forgets" all about her countertransference, because this is a subject which is understandable – but she has a subliminal fear of the patient's violence introjects.

While the patient keeps hitting with the club, the therapist's fear increases (because she feels impaired by the very loud discharge). She does not dare stop the patient and so does not have any therapeutic control of the situation.

These actual case examples from the practice should illustrate how complicated it can be to come to an indication for the use of any "therapy-enhancing" interaction objects.

The ability to use an object appropriately according to psychotherapeutic aspects of the relationship character and the transference situation can generally only be acquired by clinical case supervisions. From my own practice, I can say in general only in terms of a rule of thumb that objects should only be used as aids, if the therapist feels a certain security in the therapeutic working alliance, and if the structure of the disorder to be treated could "as a matter of principle also be otherwise" treated. The use of transitional transference objects is thus the reasonable attempt to work on the transference problem here and now in a somewhat catalyzed and partitioned way (see next section).

Therapy objects should therefore never to used out of a lack of ideas or as a rescue attempt in a completely deteriorated working relationship.

Any adequate use of an symbolizing object should in my opinion be subject to eight phases to ensure that a certain quality of the interaction performance can grow (where not all phases can always be packed into the relatively short time frame of *one therapy session*):

Phases of a Therapy Session with "Beseelte" Objects

1) *Warming up*
   Establishing contact between the individuals involved in the therapeutic work.
2) *Giving a frame*
   Determination of the previous frame of experiences, of the current subject, and of the direction of search, including clarification of the current mutual ability to work and the conditions to that end.
3) *Giving form*
   Establishing the setting, determination of the role distribution and of any particular auxiliary therapeutic instructions, e.g.: someone to hold on to for the patient, supporter for the patient, antagonist for the patient.
4) *"Beseelen"*
   Emotional attuning of the participants to the roles; establishing contact on the part of the patient with his or her inner conflict dynamics (regression or progression energy) and the external objects, as well as those involved in the roles, if applicable.
5) *Activating*
   Activating in the therapeutic roles; dynamizing of the emotional atmosphere; appropriate restoration of the conflict type and/or experimenting with the appropriate reciprocity context.
6) Resolving
   Expression of any pent-up affects and/or perception of the complex emotional atmosphere in the conflict structure, aha-experiences, evidence experiences, dissolution or loosening of all structures, and development of new structure elements as a trial solution.
7) *Specifying*
   Association of connections on different consciousness levels; finding new meanings and terms of the structure.
8) *Deriving*
   Transferring experiences into everyday life; determination of the inner structures to be protected (definition of disaster measures); deriving tasks of further development; integration of the insights gained so far; and indication of therapy perspectives.

I would like to support the foregoing by two case vignettes from Vogt (2003), since this is the best way to illustrate the specific "Beseelen" of the therapy object and the indication of the specifically developed setting derived from it:

1) Case Vignette of Patient D. – Working with a Wall Rope

Mr. D. is a 34 year old patient, who has been in an analytical body psycho-therapy for about 2 years. The therapy is about to end. When he came to me looking for a therapy, he was suffering from physical anxiety symptoms of unclear genesis, although he had already done an in-patient group therapy for two months as well as a number of individual-therapeutic sessions with different psychotherapy approaches. As a result of these therapies, he was already aware of the fact that his anxiety symptoms also had to do with the strong psychic violence communicated by his hot-tempered father and the ignorance which the latter frequently exposed in respect to his son, who apparently never succeeding in gaining his benevolent attention.

Patient D. experienced himself often as torn between a great longing for the good father, that his procreator could sometimes also be, and an extremely massive anger towards him due to the countless humiliations and denials.

During the analytical body-therapeutical interventions of the first year, many adult subjects referring to the times when he founded a new business as a freelancer and to motherly care were successfully worked on. In connection with the father transference mentioned above, however, little progress was to be noted – in relative terms. So we tried to express the innerpsychic conflict dynamics once again *in words and movements* in a session.

During the warming up phase, a movement of wanting to pull and of wanting to pull down developed in the patient. Looking for an image of the relationship, Mr. D. opted for the long thick hemp rope – and he asked me to go to the rope and to take up one end so that he could pull me through the room or pull me down. Since I was already familiar with these aggressive-sadistic impulses as a part of his father introject and also felt an active resistance to them, I modified his idea by dissociating myself from the said proposal and recommended instead attaching the end of the rope, that I would keep in my hands, to a hook cemented into the wall so that I would be able to stand still and stable on the spot and he in turn would be better able to approach the helplessness that he had suffered. The patient accepted the modified idea, because he also knew from preliminary discussions that he had never appropriately succeeded in mourning his infantile helplessness.

He then took the rope in both hands and started to pull the hemp rope jerkily. I had anchored the rope tightly and put myself in a position so that

I was directly facing Mr. D. – while holding the rope seriously – and the mounting of the hook in the wall was not visible, so that the young boy's (Mr. D. experienced himself as if he was 8 to 12 years old) tug-of-war (pulling the rope) seemed to be "quite authentic". After a few jerks he felt his old aggression again and was quickly seized with his anger affect that made him tug more and more desperately at his father, who was standing there without any relationship to him. In this connection, Mr. D. experienced *the rope as if it was the hard hand of his father.* His anger increased noticeably in view of the impossibility to move me as the therapist father or to pull me away even just half a meter or to topple me over. After about 5 minutes, the expression of anger got finally increasingly mixed with the young boy's crying, till the patient broke down in the end, crying heart-wrenchingly, while lying on the ground. At this moment, I left the role of the relationship-denying father and supported the patient by putting my hand on his shoulder.

After a few minutes of exhaustion, Mr. D. was able to say that he now had the feeling that he was in a position where he could accept the disappointed boy better, and that he now really knew what it meant "to let go".

During the subsequent follow-up discussions, the patient added that his negative parts of his father had suffered an important "defeat". In earlier times in school, he used to be a real troublemaker whom the teachers had not been able to stop. Up till then, he had not yet consciously got to know the combination that someone could be stronger than he was and still not maliciously take advantage of his superiority, which was the reason why he was so touched.

After a few additional hours, Mr. D. tried for the first time without any devastating thoughts of revenge to win his father for a heart-to-heart talk; he succeeded in doing so, and it paved the way for a certain conciliatory, but also distanced, closeness between them. The patient could control himself well in this connection, and he was also able to take the initiative for some clarifying approaches with respect to other friends, which would not have been possible for him before as the party giving in first. His self-destructive conduct with luxuries was also noticeably reduced after this episode.

Conclusion for general practice:

The structure of the setting could represent appropriately the patient's inner-psychic problems. The relationship-dynamic modification of the proposed setting by the therapist was an important corrective element for the relevance of the setting and the effect of the transitional transference object.

Based on the background of the relationship-based experience with the patient, I actively influenced the symbolized conflict pattern, and that finally opened the possibility of plunging into the patient's softer side of experience which at the same time was the relevant one in terms of changes.

The thick rope was good symbol for the patient's relationship conflict, where the point of his planned action was the dependency problem of the young boy (the longing for attention, care and love) and not the anger of revenge of the boy going through puberty or the internalized father introject (to want to defeat and to humiliate the other one again). These specifics could in fact be captured by the above activity-related performance.

After this key experience, the patient took new steps of relationship and behavior-specific corrective actions that only had to be accompanied by encouraging reflections on the part of the therapist.

2) Case Vignette of Patient B. – Working with a Giant Limp Bag and Giant Tub

Mr. B. is a young man of 25 who came to me looking for a therapy a year ago. Depressive crises, a lack of identity, authority conflicts, and a strong dependent relationship to his mother were among his main symptoms. The patient had never got to know his father; Mr. B. suffered very much under the harassments and beatings from his stepfather.

During the first year of the therapy we concentrated on stabilizing focuses. Establishing a relationship to me as a male therapist can be considered successfully achieved and the relationship as such is strong enough to be able to withstand strain. The patient no longer had any serious depressive crisis, and he reduced the contact with his mother from almost daily encounters or phone calls to monthly encounters or phone calls.

The point which could not adequately be resolved in spite of intensive psychotherapeutic work, was his *enormous fear of his stepfather* and the authority conflicts resulting from this. For that matter, there was in theory no lack of understanding of transference, of re-performance-related experiences and of experiences of violence with partially traumatizing effects. There was rather a lack of skills to implement his insights in his everyday life – or of an "effective clarification" of dysfunctional resistances.

In the therapeutic relationship I still felt then that the patient, out of fear of a loss of the relationship, was not able to show and to express any negative transference aspects towards me as his therapist father that could be really seriously felt. What was useful now and then was an analysis of slips and lapses in his dealings with me such as coming too late and similar behavioral symptoms.

The patient understood these signs "reasonably" as an expression of an unconscious aggressiveness – and couldn't still do anything about it.

At this point of stagnation, I proposed a modification of the setting that I discussed with the patient, and it helped to unravel the plot in a short time: We agreed that I as the therapist would assume specifically the stepfather's role and would "just on trial" have a look at and bear the statement of anger and the grown strength of the boy (patient B. as an adolescent going through puberty).

I did not think that any additional dynamizing clarification of the relationship was indicated, since verbal explanations and interpretations of his emotional state had been sufficiently exchanged, as described above. Furthermore, in view of early parts of the disorder of the patient, I had to reckon either with retraumatizing effects as a result of an excessive dynamization or with a pseudostabilization of his defense, so that the problem would only be pushed aside temporarily by an adjustment, only to reappear somewhere else.

For the purpose of my own physical protection, we put the giant limp bag in front of the giant tub to kick or punch into it, so that the tub was lying in front of me like a large roll. The patient could feel that his vaguely associatively and emotionally laden impression of my person was immediately changed by this setting. No further invitation was needed: fuming with rage, he started to kick against the giant bag, while he looked at me sadly and full of hatred and uttered swear words at me.

When I didn't respond to his harsh verbal attacks, he mobilized all his strength and ran against the bag and the roll and tried to push them away, which I permitted him to do, just a few centimeters. I then put myself firmly behind the roll and braked the attack. After about 8 minutes, during which the patient had kicked, punched, bawled at and cursed me, this outbreak of aggression had gone, and he said to me in quite *a different* tone that we could now stop the exercise.

During our follow-up discussion the patient said that it was the first time that he had been as loud and vigorous as was possible for him, and that he was very happy that I had not abandoned him at any moment, despite the fact that he had confronted me with such a lot of anger and swear words.

In the next session, the patient arrived on time and was highly motivated. When I asked him whether some of the anger he had expressed applied also to me, he was able to criticize some of the aspects of the reality of my relationship to him. Due to these positive new experiences, it was later much easier to exchange any negative relationship-specific experiences and fantasies, which gradually could also be implemented in the patient's environment. Recently, the patient even spoke with the head of his school because of grievances in connection with the job creation scheme project, something which before would have been unthinkable with such an authority.

During his work with the giant bag and the giant tub, the patient had also been able to see parallel to me the real image of his stepfather and to re-experience again his helplessness as a boy, as he later explained *in the second subsequent lesson* (see above).

He said that he had never before experienced so consciously such a strong anger and grief, which helped him to find a relieving expression of his feelings.

Furthermore, the patient also found that the slack bag lying in front of the tub also matched well the image of his family, where his weak mother had always also defended the brutal stepfather. This interpretation helped him in the following weeks, too, to establish better boundaries with respect to his mother.

Therapeutic Conclusion:

The performance enabled an important therapeutic progress. The symbolizing objects used had the quality of transitional transference objects, according to the above definition. Bag and tub represented both the negative transference sides of the real stepfather figure, who had previously only been dealt with rationally, as well as the negative partial objects of the therapist, and could evidently be connected with the patient's transference-related perceptions in an emotionally sensible way due to the said symbolization.

That the "therapist father was ready to come to meet the son or willing to make concessions and to leave his habitual setting" was, of course, also a fact that was important for the successful setting.

Ultimately, this use of an object had a triangulating effect in the deadlocked dialogue, because it allowed the patient to be *at the same time in and beside* the affect in a suitable way, thereby giving him the possibility of observing emotions in an experienceable context and to abstractly comprehend and to verbalize them without any excessive risk of loss regarding the relationship.

As a consequence thereof, the therapeutic work became more holistic and for the patient more active in terms of actions (see Vogt, 2002 b).

The above case vignettes show in the indication-specific situation how transitional transference objects can be created in the therapeutic relationship, and what effect they can have. The therapy aids described above mainly fulfilled two functions: On the one hand, they facilitated the technical performance of the therapeutic activity-related experiments by giving the participants the possibility of an interaction that could relative easily be carried out physically and that emphasized the essentials of the problem felt, and at the same time helped to find an optimum balance between closeness and distance in the therapeutic work.

On the other hand, these objects become transitional transference objects because their use, based on the psychotherapeutic transference, is consciously reflected by the patient in his way and "beseelt" at the moment of the activity-related performance.

1.3.2 The Approach of Relational Analysis-Based Work on Transference

The term transference in its clinical-psychological application has on the one hand been interpreted very broadly and with some variation (see Laplanche and Pontalis, 1991, p. 550 ff) – but on the other hand, we can confine ourselves here to its psychoanalytical interpretations (see Arnold, Eysenck, Meili, 1993, p. 2384/2385).

According to my understanding, the authors are in agreement that transferences refer to processes where an innerpsychic and/or an external behavioral problem of an individual can be explained to a great extent out of a non-resolved psycho-dynamic event and/or conflict situation that might be responsible for the unmastered experience and the inefficient behavior of the individual.

That means that the client transfers the bad experiences or the unresolved component of the experienced conflict type to new situation and relationship constellations, so that in the end he or she recognizes them again within the framework of his or her projections, or his or her previous experiences flash up with a labilizing effect as a result thereof; or by actively restoring them within the framework of projective identifications, or by letting himself or herself maneuver again into the previous unmastered problem situation.

In analytical literature such a relapse and recurrence or repetition is referred to as regression (see also the reference works mentioned above); the result of such psycho-dynamic procedures are behavioral fixations, misbehaviors in the current situation, or a promotion of conditions for self-damaging retraumatizations.

Geißler (2001) presents a very comprehensive overview of the conceptual use of regression or of the variety of interpretations of treatment concepts, from analytical and body psychotherapy of the last century up to today. Of special interest in this connection are new regression concepts describing the active and also healthy interaction of the different regulating levels in the individual under the keyword of "Modern Infant Research". Stern's modern regression concept which basically purports that it is not the "whole" individual which inevitably relapses to earlier development stages, but that only partial and momentary losses of the often present competency of self-regulation occur under specific (labilizing) conditions, a concept which was also taken up by Bocian and Staemmler (2000).

I can certainly go along with these statements, would, like to design, however, just the following organization matrix in terms of my own structural approach, since my specific use of transitions transference objects also refers to this matrix:

Table 1:

Therapist's experience				
		A	B	C
		NCT	MCT	PCT
1	NT	1A	1B	1C
2	MT	2A	2B	2C
3	PT	3A	3B	3C

(Patient's experience — left vertical axis)

Matrix of transferences

1) NT=Negative transference of the patient
2) MT=Mixed transference of the patient
3) PT=Positive transference of the patient

A) NCT=Negativ countertransference of the patient
B) MCT=Mixed countertransference of the patient
C) PCT=Positive countertransference of the patient

1) A transference comprises at least the following combinations as a result of the specific personalities of the patient and the therapist:

a) Properties, based on which the interaction partners re-experience the really disturbed sides of the other partner according to his or her *earlier negative experiences.*
b) Particularities, based on which the interaction partners re-experience only similarities with such earlier negative experiences (mixed transferences).
c) Chances, based on which the interaction partners can discover new sides of the other partner, as opposed to their previous experiences.

2) Transferences and countertransferences can occur in the form of at least three different perception levels in the interaction of a relationship:

a) as similarities with the *characteristic properties* of a person;
b) as similarities of a type of interaction in a specific situation; or
c) as similarities of *atmospheric conditions of a reciprocal effect* as a frame of a disturbed perception.

Neither the classical analytical nor the bioenergetic-body-therapeutic nor another approach takes account of this diversity of transference possibilities in the design of the setting and in the conception of the therapy, according to my point of view.

In my opinion, however, it is worthwhile to tap into various transference capacities. This would mean that a greater transference diversity could be created and more transference modulation could be established experimentally. I feel that the therapy situation should be seen as a chance to express the patient's difficult emotions in a dosed performance and to resolve them in a way on the spot – in the presence of the therapist.

But to that end, the classical analytical setting does not, in my view, approach the center point or the intersection of the performance courageously and actively enough. The establishment of transferences and sometimes of a transference neurosis is observed with a lot of sensitivity and also verbally dealt with; but apart from the factor of the development time (catching up on maturation) and of the interpretation of the transference situation, there is no further possibility of exerting any influence. As an *analytical therapist* I cannot, for example, in the case of any transference resistance, actively do anything – apart from the (imposed) waiting, inquiring or "suggesting" – in order to "bring" a transference situation "into" the analytical session.

Although *body-oriented colleagues* of other therapy schools come to the point of action quicker, with respect to the relationship, however, there is not always a guarantee that the problem performed really does adequately represent the most difficult and most important emotional relationship-specific dilemma of the patient, because the transference constellations are not fully checked or reviewed in the current relationship here and now. On the other hand, *psychodynamically working colleagues* do not shrink from updating the complicated relationship performance; here, however, a great pressure can quickly be brought about on the part of the patient that enhances a re-traumatizing escalation of the transference-related performance.

While previous approaches of analytical psychotherapy concentrated very much on the standard situation of the main relationship-specific work referred to in the interaction field 1C (see Freud, 1920), with the beginning of the 1950s the focus shifted to a stronger emphasis being put on the resistence sides of the therapist (see Racker, 1959) or on the fertile analytical work with the concept of countertransference.

Bettighofer (1998) goes one step further in his process-dynamical analysis approach of transference and countertransference by postulating that negative transference would not only be inevitable but should also be enhanced within the framework of an *active confrontation* – by maintaining the analytical setting. In the area of body psychotherapy, Heinrich (2001) sees chances of actively acting out a transference and countertransference in a process-oriented body work, which avoids any interpreting procedure (p. 62 ff., ibid.).

I would like to add here – as already in Vogt (2002, b) – as a focus of psychotherapeutic work the aspect of a *conscious modulation and modification of transferences* within the framework of a maximally wide range of modulation.

What I mean in this connection is that we should strive within the framework of our therapeutic work to *consciously establish* various transference situations, if they have a natural and specific relevance for the patient, and to represent them with regard to the different aspects, in order

1) to make transferences visible through modulation and thereby diagnosable for the patient;
2) to demonstrate the variability of transferences through the therapist's active involvement in the relationship (mutual character and the like) and to encourage that transferences are actively coped with;
3) to create here and now resolution examples with the patient for a reduction of the transference; and
4) and also to create better possibilities for a reduction of his or her countertransferences.

According to my point of view and conception, such a working style is most easily made possible within the framework of performances with transitional transference objects being used as symbolizing objects for a vivid representation of the constellations of neuroses and as aids for a therapeutic development of the relationship (see above section 1.3.1).

As a result, any work *on the transference* – i.e. proceeding with relatively little dynamizing – will become the determining target direction and in terms of tendency the developmental frame of the therapeutic relationship structure.

On the other hand, such a trilogical object approach also provides the possibility of at certain points less burdened analytical work *in the transference*, if e.g. transference and countertransference have to be acted out on a short-term basis between the patient and the therapist, in order to restore the ability of work on the basic relationship (see case example Sven Reimann under 2.1.2).

While the therapeutic modification of the relationship developed from 1C to 3C in the classical approach of psychoanalysis (see Matrix of Transferences above) and the modifications shifted in later developmental stages of this psychotherapy from 1B to 3B, with this approach I am trying to point out that still more of the difficult cases of column A or the special cases from 1 to 3A or from 1 to 3B will be included for the therapist in the developmental work of the relationship, by also giving the therapist a chance of expressing his or her inner emotional state in a therapeutical object-based interaction with the client or sometimes also prior to the client.

Since this interaction is psychologically founded and this kind of action is used to make the relationship-specific problems visible, the result is a psychotherapeutic reference frame and an affectively-impressive relationship benefit which adds awareness and authenticity to the situation in the model scene.

In the movement proposals of bioenergetic therapists or concentrative movement therapists I see a similar attempt that concentrates on the developmental forms of the relationship; in my opinion, they remain, however, in terms of their practical performance, more attached to the "transference triangle" 3B-2C-3C, because they do not actively interfere in the movement scene *with their countertransference.*

A second thesis regarding the modification of the transference work with transitional transference objects assumes that such transference forms which the patient experiences as problematic, but which he or she so far could not perceive and work on due to the limited projection of the therapist, should also be explicitly checked or reviewed in the therapy (and hence also be established on a short-term basis). Here, an object or an object constellation takes over the "triggering" of 1A, 2A, 1B, and 2B during the action. This would also provide the possibility of better work *on* the transference.

Ultimately, I find that the preposition *on* is also a bit misleading, because a "vividly experienced" *transference* also always triggers a feeling of being *in the transference.* And when I am in an analytical therapy session in the transference with a patient and talk about previous experiences with his or her parents, I am in the end also "outside" again and work *on the transference.*

In this context I think it would be entirely more appropriate if we spoke of the target maxim of working **in** *a vivid transference interaction process* **on** *a descriptive transference object.*

The point is always an effective setting in which the patient can recognize the evidence of his transference in the therapy session and resolve it.

The aim of this section will have been achieved, if I have succeeded in adequately pointing out here that the approach of the structural universal psychotherapy focuses on a less relationship-dynamizing but still a very authentic and wide-ranging representation of transference problems in the movement with the aid of objects. The main contribution is considered to be not only the interpretation of the transference, but rather the *modification of the transference* on the spot in one and the same therapy session as a model for a new relationship experience.

1.3.3 The Concept of the Dynamic Unity of Introject and Transference

1.3.3.1 The Introject and the Dynamic of Reciprocity in the Dynamic Introject Transference Scheme

In psychoanalytic literature far less has been written about the term of the introject than about the term of transference. I think one reason for this might be that "internalized" objects have been associated more with the voluntarily identified and thus less influenceable parts of a personality (see Laplanche and Pontalis, 1991, p. 235 ff. or Arnold, Eysenck, Meili, 1993, p. 1018).

In this context, the subject is dealt with by drawing a line from fantasized incorporations of an object by the child – for an extended need fulfillment, so to speak – up to the defense of inner frustrations by adoption of the outside world (see above authors, ibid.).

If Wolpe's statements (in Arnold, Eysenck, Meili, 1993, p. 1474 ff.) regarding the development of the properties of neuroses are also taken into consideration, one might add that an important part of the behaviors (introjects) that have been internalized by the child are habitual behaviors of the influential attachment figures and which were adopted by the child as a model. There are also differences in the opinions regarding the correlation between introjections and projections.

Ferenczi, who introduced the term *introjection* in 1909 (see Laplanche and Pontalis, 1991, p. 235/239), described its psychodynamic relevance as the opposite of the defense mechanism of *projection*, which ultimately are both allocated to the general term of transference. The metaphor of "transference addiction" used by Ferenczi appears to be problematic only to the extent that too much of a "defense profit" is attributed to the child making transferences on the level of a transfer-to-the-inside-or-to-the-outside. In my view, this is, however, only one side of what happens here, and with such a strictly one-dimensional point of view it can again lead to the postulate of the "child-himself-causing-the-neurosis".

The majority of the Freudian – and later, in particular, also of the Kleinian – explanation concepts in psychoanalysis (see Freud, Collected Works, Vol. I, 1969; Klein, 1932, 1962; Mahler et al., 1980) see the child as the drive-controlled and wish-controlled originator causing his or her own conflicts by passively experiencing his or her environment and unconsciously acting with the environment. According to these authors, neurotic projections and introjections could only be given up by a *conscious adaptation of the child* to his or her adult living world. Basically, that means that a child could become the *actual perpetrator* in the dynamics of his or her neurosis with a *healthier living environment.*

The old paradigm of psychoanalysis could only be reformed after the results of Modern Infant Research were available (see Stern, 1991, 1996; Lichtenberg, 1991; Dornes, 1997, 1998, 2002a; Downing, 1996; Geißler, 1998, 2002, 2003).

These researchers and analytical experts have furnished impressive evidence that children are firstly much more active when it comes to the acquisition of relationship experiences, and that they are secondly also much more at the mercy of early shaping forms of an affect-motor interaction than we dared to believe before.

Bad relationship experiences are much more sustainably retained in the subliminal communication style of the individual and unconsciously shape new relationship-specific perceptions and development patterns than had been previously assumed.

That means that one reason why neurotic transferences sometimes have such a tenacious effect in the treatment of an adult is that they were *also shaped and anchored so early as an introject in the communication style.* The transferences that are revealed in the relationship-specific behavior of the individual have only to a limited extent something to do with rememberable conflicts because certain affect-motor schemes are difficult to access on a conscious level. The explanations that we have in respect to our behavior communicate key points of the disorder genesis; they are not, however, the "whole and pure cause as such". That means, for example, that even in Freud's time the sexual drive should not have been the major cause of infantile neuroses, but only *one major explanation*, because the subject of and dealing with sexuality was a great societal problem at the turn of the last century.

The dynamic of a sexual taboo determined by Freud "from the couch" – accompanied at the same time by sexual activities in society in the form of affairs with acquaintances, rapes in everyday life and in marriages, sexual abuse of adolescents, and incest in the family, and the like – was obviously so strong that it was evidently "too terrifying and no longer conceivable" for Freud that it would be possible for him to drain this huge swamp of societal disorders. He thus early opted for an *explanation concept of disordered children with respective complexes*, so as to ensure, possibly, that his work could continue to be tolerable at all. Otherwise a handful of analysts would hardly have received the societal legitimation to uncover the perceptible psychosocial misery at the turn of the last century; they were already then faced with enormous hostilities just because of the *sexual drive theory in childhood development.*

Be that as it may, the problem of the "negative forces" in the psychic development of the child has currently reached a new status of discussion where the point is neither a generalized demonization of the living conditions nor a prejudgment of the parents or any other guardians, but to make aware of the complicated reciprocities that exist between *active but at the same time complexly dependent and determined individuals* who are subject to the psychodynamic mechanisms of *both* introjections and projections.

Analytical resistance concepts such as that of the "negative therapeutic reaction" (see Mertens, 1993, p. 175-191) raise the question again and again as to which projected or introjected forces would suddenly like to thwart the success of the psychotherapeutic treatment? One might think that a therapeutically changed individual – a change just brought about in a good therapy session – ought to be quite interested in further recovery. In Mertens (ibid. p. 191) that analyst again concludes that there must be serious character disorders on the part of the patient causing fear and despair in him that *his former introjects* could be destroyed (emphasis by the author). Does that mean that the patient established this all by himself with his unchangeable character disorders? I feel this is a biased fatal interpretation of an infantile self-causation.

When trying to explain such negative relationship forces, I think it is absolutely necessary to draw more upon the *dynamics of subliminal introjects in relationship to near-conscious projections (transferences).* These introjects especially refer to *involuntarily* adopted, i.e. not consciously identified, habitual external objects, which were adopted up to the point that such an adoption was made out of (an existential) fear under serious psychic pressure – with a shaping effect on the psychic. In connection with such theoretical considerations I feel that we can lean on modern trauma research where these dynamics have been described in connection with the internalization of the introjects of perpetrators by victims of violence and where the classical approach of the "neurotic child in a healthy environment" has also been vehemently rejected (see Huber, 2003 a, b, chapters 2 to 5).

Based on my long-standing experience with averagely damaged neurosis patients, I feel that the basic patterns of an involuntary internalization of object experiences are also to be found here. Although it is true that the introject patterns show in a less dissociated and split form, they are, however, not less long-lived and are tenaciously effective.

When I was not yet so experienced in walk-in psychotherapy, I sometimes hastily dismissed such cases of unexpected "backward fluctuations and obvious similarities with parents" as "that is just so contradictory or just inherited". That is not exactly how I see it anymore.

Due to self-experienced patients with a very good introspection capability and trauma patients I was able to collect examples that show how a sudden break-through of an introject is brought about or under which psychically burdensome circumstances a dimension of very problematic introjects emerged (see case examples under 2.1.1.1; 2.1.2.1; 2.1.3.1 and 2.1.4.1). It is apparently so that introjects of the complicated negative – often self-destructive – form are also brought about under considerable inner-psychic stress of the child. In the cases of these examples of existential need, of permanent helplessness towards an important reference person or attachment figure, the child was no match. The child has the feeling of being completely dependent on this reference person or attachment figure and is at the same time enormously afraid of not being able to live up to the expectations of these individuals or of losing still more "the favor of the impairing object". Or the child clings to the incompetent adult because he loves this adult very much and believes himself to be unable to live on without the adult. According to my collection of cases, such violence-laden and/or heart-wrenching emotional ambivalences very soon give rise to very complicated negative introjects of these tormentors that want to interfere continuously with the treatment.

The thesis of a broad unconscious development of early introjects due to the reference persons or attachment figures the child experiences has also been underlined by the reflections of Dornes (2000 and 2002 b), where he provides analytical examples which demonstrate how even observed behavior is reflected and internalized by the child.

That means that we probably really have to assume that everything experienced by a small child is already internalized as "the whole scene with the distribution of all roles", whether we like it or not. Of course, not everything will be effective to the same degree, but rather potentially available and possible. The weighing and importance of the "inner filing" will – at first unconsciously – be dynamically determined. The performance of all distributed roles seems to work in such a way that the re-establishment of the experienced circumstances is on the one hand transferred to the outside to new environments – and that on the other hand it also has an impact on the inside in terms of a (never-ending) self-performance between transference and introject.

This makes psychotherapy, of course, very complicated, because transferences and introjects work to the same extent to the outside in shaping the relationship to the environment – as well as they work together and against each other to the inside within the acquired relationship to oneself. Specifically this means, for example, that one succeeded in a psychotherapy session in working on a relationship and in bringing about a good relationship-specific change in the "new family" of the patient, but that this change is then brought down again by an old introject in the patient himself. Under unfavorable circumstances this will in turn not be reflected in the next therapy situation, because a "transference child" will be sitting here again. Or the patient's inner interplay was worked on well – and when the patient visits his "old family", everything will be toppled over again in terms of the style of the old regression, because the patient will be set back excessively (due to triggers) by the introject style of the reference persons or attachment figures (a contact with the perpetrator, so to speak, in terms of trauma research) and the framework of the transference of the long-known family roles.

I think that in both respects there is still additional analysis required. A lot of work has been done in respect to transferences, but what is the current and still real effect of existing introject influences on the patient here and now in his or her situation in life? That means: Where is the patient correct in assuming that he is still damaged in terms of the style of the old introjects, because there is no transference? And where has he not quite understood that he continues to greatly impair himself in terms of the style of the old introjects?

I call the concept of the condition of transference and introject properties regenerating itself reciprocally, as a relatively balanced interactional regulation a *Dynamic Transference Introject Scheme*. In order to avoid any excessive extensions of terms and to simplify matters, I refer to the majority of regressed properties as transference and to the majority of neurosis-progressed moments in connection with a neurotic performance as introject.

First, that means that I consider it as a transference experience in a narrower sense if someone slides into a psychic state where he gets into a role which he experienced as impairing in his childhood and loses in connection with these inner-psychic responses a certain level of his adult competences. Sometimes he will be reactive-passive in his perception of himself and of others – or he acts because he fails to see any adequate possibility of coping with the situation, with the risk of a damage to self or foreign objects becoming chronic.

This means in addition that I consider it as an introject experience in a narrower sense if someone gets into a psychic state in which he performs a role which he experienced as impairing in his childhood and destroys a certain level of his adult competences in connection with these inner-psychic actions. Sometimes he will be reflexive in his aliented self-perception – or because he fails to adequately assess the situation, he acts actively in a self-damaging and chronifying way in terms of the old and non-ego determination of the situation.

That means that this *Dynamic Transference Introject Scheme* works, for example, as if the degrading parents would now still be talking insistently to the meantime 30 year old boy: But as a patient the boy first perceives his transferences at best and possibly considers the therapist as the latent degrader. If he is then, however, upgraded by the therapist in a certain therapy situation, the patient – as introject of his parents – must suddenly degrade himself heavily. If the therapist then in turn talks of this repetition, the patient will possibly feel criticized again (and not cared for) because of this extended information, and he then experiences the therapist again in the well-known transference as a parent, whom he could never please. If the therapist subsequently interprets this circle of interaction, the patient will feel exposed, equalling another aggravation of this relationship disorder, and will progress even further into the regressive transference – or he will possibly contradict vigorously and think in terms of the neurosis-identified (self-damaging) introject that the therapist is right and that he, the patient, just does so many things wrong in therapy – as in life – and has only himself to blame for his self-esteem deficit, etc.

This tiny case vignette is supposed to outline how circuitously such transference introject dialogues can develop. An analytical colleague would now work on this process by means of stories and interpretations, meta-cognitions and metaphors; however, I also use another method for bringing the dynamic reciprocities vividly to the mind, which I refer to as introject transference role plays. Based on this I try to show the inner-psychic impact of transference and introject sides by referring to healthy parts of the patient and to establish the boundary in respect to the main characters who had a shaping effect in early childhood. This will be explained in the next section.

In preparation for the structural psychotherapeutic work and the role plays which are to follow later, I ask each patient somewhere between about the 10th and 20th session to prepare a table of the currently conscious major transferences and major introjects of his or her most important guardians. The sentences which are to be entered are discussed together on the basis of the following *questions* and finally included in the table as currently valid working hypotheses (see chart):

Table 2:

	Transference	Introject
Mother	Which property/action-related disposition of your mother bothered/did harm to you in particular as a child so that you today still relapse quickly – also among strangers – into your old infantile/juvenile emotional world/need?	Which similar property/action-related disposition of your mother do you have today – whether or not you want this consciously or only notice it now and then ashamedly/are told it now and then, so that you in turn (might) impair yourself or others with it?
Father	Correspondingly for the father.	Correspondingly for the father.
Other person	Correspondingly for this person.	Correspondingly for this person.

The aim is to enter any important major transferences or major introjects hierarchically into this table and to check their relevance on a quarterly basis, because the accents can change successively according to the therapeutic treatment phases and often also the order of rank. The size of the table depends on the number of the persons having an impact on the individual. Such "other persons" often refer to a grandma, a grandpa, with whom the patients lived a long time during their childhood; an older sister or brother who had an upbringing influence in the family; an uncle as a substitute for a non-available or non-existing father; step-parents, and many more. These are individuals who had considerable influence on the development of the child and who are likely to have been decisive for the structure of the major symptoms.

1.3.3.2 Structure of Introject Transference Role Plays as a Therapy Approach

In our joint practice, introject transference role play performances proved especially useful for an intensive work on the Dynamic Transference Introject Schemes.

The advantage of this approach is certainly the very vivid didactic creative process for the patient which we generally pursue in structural therapy. The aim is that the patient should as far as possible be a mature auxiliary therapist and learn to perform his inner-psychic performances by himself and to work on them, of course, with a high degree of activity on his own, as it is required by role plays anyway, in order to improve his ability to differentiate so far until he has reached an adequate level of a healthier self-control.

The core is putting the inner-psychic roles of the patient opposite to each other according to the following principle:

Graph 7: Model of the Dynamic Introject Transference Role Play Scheme of the fictive patient Max Müller:

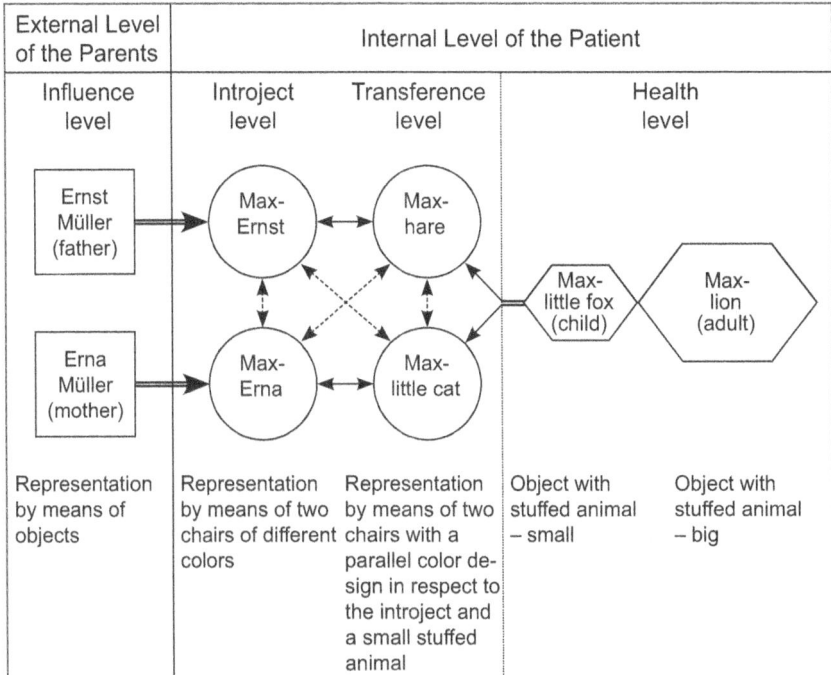

External Level of the Parents	Internal Level of the Patient		
Influence level	Introject level	Transference level	Health level
Ernst Müller (father)	Max-Ernst	Max-hare	Max-little fox (child) Max-lion (adult)
Erna Müller (mother)	Max-Erna	Max-little cat	
Representation by means of objects	Representation by means of two chairs of different colors	Representation by means of two chairs with a parallel color design in respect to the introject and a small stuffed animal	Object with stuffed animal – small Object with stuffed animal – big

When these roles have been confronted in such a construction, an important diagnostic step has already been accomplished for the patient, because the patient must try to transform his or her inner psychic perception and regulation levels into symbolized figures. This will, of course, also be accompanied by resistances which are, however, important for diagnostic reasons and partially reveal the patient's weakness to differentiate. It will in any case be helpful and enhance the structural development, if the therapist provides explorative support here, e.g. when the client thinks that he has no healthy parts at all etc. In this case, the therapist should benevolently and firmly ask whether there are any exceptions in this respect. The same applies to representations of any transference effects on the child. From my point of view, it is important in this case that the patient concentrates on the main effects of how he felt as a child towards the influencing parent when he found himself in any regressive states, and what he became symbolically as a result of the numerous responses in connection with this problem.

On the introject level there is usually the particular problem that it is difficult for patients to differentiate between the attitudes of the parents and the internalized sides thereof – i.e. what they really say to themselves or how they treat themselves. It is also an impressive diagnostic progress, if patients notice these conceptual mixtures and gain a vivid impression of the term "introject".

If the first phase of this constellation diagnosis has been exhausted, the role identification phase will follow next where the specific positions and emotions of the different representative figures (e.h. mother transference and father transference, as well as mother introject and father introject) are captured. Here the patient will again have various difficulties to engage in some of the differentiated roles, while he will feel quickly very comfortable in other roles. These aspects are also didactically valuable in therapy.

The representation of the reciprocities between the representative figures begins in a third step, where any parallel and cross perceptions, as well as the relationship patterns between the transference introject levels play a vital role.

Here, the therapist intervenes as a coordinating questioner and helps to work out the problem of relationship conflicts. The interview style is marked by open questions and later includes more and more the health levels and the external influence levels.

During the last phase any new formations of the representation image are reviewed experimentally. For example, the patient suddenly changes the representation variants of the stuffed animals or objects in the next session, because he or she experiences a symbol as "no longer really suitable" (indirect cognition), or because he or she brings a conscious insight into the image (direct cognition).

This also happens due to contradictions which are pointed out by the interviewing therapist. It often becomes apparent that transference objects are inner-psychically held in check and prevented from developing by negative introjects. Basically these inner-neurotic dynamics work only because precisely the *healthy* child and adult levels have too little influence on this homeostatic reciprocity (see example ibid.). This role play setting comes to an end, at least for the time being, if and when the introject figures "return" their negative order and express a symbolic acceptance in respect to the "transference children". A more detailed description of the role play theory will be presented in a later publication, since this would go beyond the concerns of this book.

1.3.3.3 Structure of Introject General Role Plays and of Other Performance Settings

Here I will give only a short theoretical outline as to which kind of role play conceptions I consider to be included in the approach of structural universal psychotherapy; more detailed presentations of the concepts will be published later.

I consider the *"Family Dynamic Introject Generation Scheme"* an important supplement of the foregoing Dynamic Introject Transference Scheme, because the massiveness of the above-mentioned introjects sometimes cannot be worked on adequately by merely working on the *inner-psychic dynamics*. But also sometimes real family members interfere actively in the patient's therapy at a certain time and slow the process down. Or, as a result of dreams and other unconscious or emotional resistance blockades, situations are brought about in the client which could not be adequately worked on with the prevailing means and methods.

In this case I think "that the introjects must have more space to be understood". In his childhood, the patient often paid much attention to the problems of his parents and was willing to make concessions or to accommodate to that end so that his "installed introjects vigorously oppose any discharge from their task".

Practically, this means that I try to meet the resistance exactly there where it is emotionally working internally at that moment: The child often "wanted" to solve the problems of his parents so that the child "may" now in the role play really once "truly understand" the problem play of his parent "and to play it to the end". The parent concerned could also have been better available to his or her child – or could have avoided impairing the child excessively if the parent had worked on his or her own conflict neurosis in connection with his or her own parents (the present grandparents). The aim here is to reveal without any fears, taboos, and false consideration in the place of the parent the facts clarifying the relationship.

The following model helps to illustrate this context:

Graph 8: Dynamic Generation Introject Scheme: The role plays take place first in field A and then in field B – or the other way around, depending on urgency.

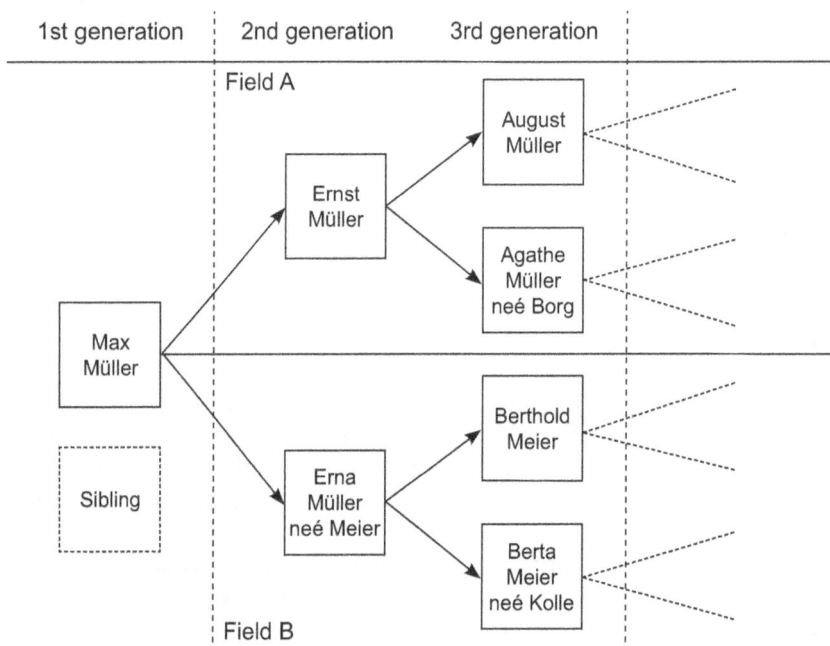

The advantage of this concept is that the "infantile mind" comes rest better this way and also that the transmission of the introject is thus demonstrated vividly. Since in this way the introject in the influencing reference persons can also be seen and worked on accordingly, the introject pressure will also be reduced in the emotional circle of the patient which is being acted out.

During the first phase of the role play the patient describes what he suffered from, in particular, in connection with his reference persons and then continues to track down the chain of hurts to conflicts prevailing among older generations – prior to his birth.

The main difference to the procedure of Pesso (1986) and Moreno (1946) is that the structures are strongly aligned to the psychological dimensions of the transference and of the introject and that the problematic negative psychodynamic contexts are to be made visible which the patient would otherwise not confront himself, because in role play approaches he naturally tends to represent his problems only as (resolvable) real or ideal behavior. Yet, in the non-dismantled role structures of the psychodrama, the "introjects will also play a part in the old manner in the role of the negative father and the like, which can ultimately lead to latent retraumatizations. Furthermore, introjects will become more firmly established by any undifferentiated repetition or overly quick solution of the patient, for example, if he only scolds his parents in an affective dramaturgy, and so basically "forgets" to work on his introjects with which he is, for example, already impairing his own children. In Pesso's approach, the conflict side gets lost, i.e. what the client should play, if he is (today) not just seeking (does not need) ideal parents but instead at first has to develop the ability to finally establish boundaries autonomously or aggressively.

On the other hand, in psychotherapy, of course, we also need both these well-known and other forms of role plays which in conclusion I would like to only summarize and to refer you to future, more detailed publications.

In the structural universal psychotherapy approach hierarchical and typical disorder-specific indications are decisive for the selection of the role play setting. Below you will find a list of the most frequent role play options in an empirical order together with a corresponding explanation:

Role play structures in general sequence

1) *Diagnostic episode role plays*

   These are used in individual therapy or mostly in group therapy to represent the authentic relationships of the patient with the most important persons influencing the patient (usually family members).

   The patient is to enact a typical model situation which has left an influential emotional impression of these persons.

2) *Statement role plays*

   In this situation the patient, whose psychic development conditions are well-known in the individual or group therapy, is given the opportunity to confront the impairing parent without any fears, taboos or false consideration in order to release himself from any pent-up affects and to open himself up to new resolution attempts.

3) *Diagnostic family constellations*

   Here the patient demonstrates by means of objects, stuffed animals and the like how the relationships were in his original family, and tries to comprehend with the help of the therapist's circular questioning the family's motives in terms of their emotional states, perceptions, and actions against the background of their reciprocal effects.

4) *Introject transference role plays*

   These are designed to illustrate the inner-psychic reciprocal dynamics of introject and transference in the patient and their impact on self-regulation. (see "Concept" above.)

5) *Generation introject role plays*

They are designed to illustrate the reciprocal dynamics and the transmission of the introjects across generations within the family, up to the impact on the patient's self-regulation. (see "Concept" above.)

6) *Model role plays of the healthier child*

Here the patient tries out how a less impaired child could have behaved under approximately the same living conditions, if there had been any appropriate supporters besides the family.

7) *Real role plays of the healthier adult*

Here the patient tests how he can as an adult deal with the persons who still exist and are impairing him or how he could have dealt differently with those negative influencers who are dead.

8) *Real role plays of the healthier adult in conflicts of everyday life*

Here the patient attempts to comprehend the specific emotional relationship situation and to respond most favorably within the framework of his possibilities or to initiate a cooperative and/or consistent discussion.

These eight steps of a role play concept often build up on each other in a series of steps. But depending on the indication the order can also be different. The above sequence corresponds to the empirical experiences I have had so far.

Of course, there may also be leaps and repetitions during the role play performances. The only important thing from my point of view is that the structure of role plays has been reasonably discussed and derived with the patient so that he understands the point. The effect of role play scenarios is often impaired by the fact that only the therapist understands why this model should now be used purposefully or that only the patient determines what should be an important role model at the moment. However, psychotherapeutic relationship diagnostics are required everywhere. The structure of the role play derivations must present the emotionally most important focus and resistance point of the present therapy in the form of scenes.

1.3.4 The Concept of Using Self-Designed Therapy Material of Patients (Texts, Drawings, Sculptures)

In this section I want to just briefly outline how the fact that the structural work of a universal psychotherapy also extends to any self-designed work of the patient which is produced outside of the therapy sessions.

Preliminary work and post-session evaluation are equally important both for the patient and the therapist in order to ensure that any perception differences, changes of interpretations, or alterations of the target are noticed early within the framework of the therapeutic work and can be included in the therapy process. It is not a rare occurrence that transference or introject-related problems become evident in small behavior sequences or fantasies before or after a therapy session, and these need to be noticed. Another point is that it is important that the patient becomes his "own research expert" very early and develops an active interest in his diagnosis and therapy, in keeping with the conceptual statements made above.

The patient will be set the following tasks:

A) Therapy diary

Each patient is required to keep a special therapy diary in which dreams between the therapy sessions and thoughts before and after the therapy sessions are to be recorded. In addition, any important blockade points or insights of the patient are to be entered in the diary, since they otherwise might disappear immediately again if they are not recorded at once. Therefore, keywords can therefore also be recorded during the therapy session. These relative short therapy process diaries will almost always contribute to a more independent self-analysis. It is frequently impressive for the clients to comprehend their extremely different self-assessments and assessments of situations in a time-lapse, which will also enhance the development of structure.

B) Therapy drawings

Within the framework of structural psychotherapy each patient is given the sometimes optional task of producing drawings with painting colors or wax crayons according to his moods and emotions (a format between A5 and A1 can be freely chosen). The pictures which he brings along with him to the therapy sessions are evaluated at the beginning of a therapy session in three phases:

1) Interpretation on the basis of the patient's intention

Here the patient can explain anything he thought or felt when he produced the drawing, what the purpose or aim of the drawing was or what he had in mind that the therapist should see "in any case", etc. In this first phase everything may be explained.

The first spontaneous statements of three selected patients with regard to their motives were according to my records as follows (see pictures in the annex under 4.2):

Patient A:
"I would like to find my center, but everything is turning around too quickly."

Patient B:
"As a boy I can't accomplish anything between mother and father, and I
could just vomit."

Patient C:
"With the therapist, I feel safe like with a good grandfather, and I swing frisk-
ily."

2) Interpretation as a wanderer
Here the patient is asked to make an effort to learn to view his drawing once
with a neutral distance – like a stranger. Here the spontaneous, vaguely associatively and emotionally laden impression of the accidental beholder is
in the foreground. Because this perspective is difficult for most patients at
the beginning, here the therapist also expresses some spontaneous ideas that
come to his mind – without any apparent therapeutical purpose except to
divert the patient and to lead him away from any "serious interpretation" in
order to lighten up what can often be a tense situation during the search for
a meaning (see also the pictures under 4.2).

In the case examples of the above-mentioned patients A, B, and C the
statements of the wanderer were as follows:

Patient A:
"A pretty, colored windwheel."
Therapist:
"Like the pupil of an eye or a fire flue."

Patient B:
"A child is being crushed there in a monster forest."
Therapist:
"The bubbling fountain at the head of the boy is an eternal spring for the
others."

Patient C:
"A nursery school for adults."
Therapist:
"The child in a man never gets old."

The advantage of such spontaneous, arbitrary, and not very purposeful statements is often a better distancing from the (fixed) emotional content, which makes it possible to deal with the most difficult problems in a relaxed – sometimes even humorous – way, which is basically something needed at times in all therapeutic work. Furthermore it trains a "stranger's view" of things, which means that the patient learns a decentralized way of thinking and feeling in respect to his or her environment, so that he or she will better be able to withstand any (disturbing) accidental influences on the part of others.

3) Interpretation as an auxiliary therapist
Here the patient is asked to deliberately assume a therapeutic attitude towards himself for a while and to evaluate what he would think or what fantasies he would have in connection with this drawing about the patient X, if *he* would see this drawing *as a therapist*.

Of course, the respective therapy phase (and previous sculptures) also have to be taken into consideration here.

Since this "foreign view" is also difficult for the client at the beginning, I help the patient as a therapist by enhancing such empathic ideas by associations of my own.

A positive effect on the level of the relationship is also that negative transference aspects can be reduced "by the way" in this connection, so to speak, since patient and therapist can deal with each other on the "level of colleagues" and can easily talk shop. And this will again generate more distanced serious as well as slightly humorous statements and views.

As examples I would like to present here the following statements of the above-mentioned patients A, B, and C from an auxiliary therapeutic view regarding the drawings in the annex (see annex, under 4.2):

Patient A:
"A human being is not yet visible. Client X is afraid of his own feelings and needs to have confidence."
Therapist:
"Client X experiences strong inner forces which might consist of longing and aggression. Any emotions are obviously controlled through a big control eye. This is, however, strenuous for him."

Patient B:
"Client X is in an infantile phase at the moment and is re-experiencing his helplessness between his parents once again."
Therapist:

61

"Client X reveals his distress as a single child as well as the massive disorder of his parents, which he was not allowed to do so far. That is a good start."

Patient C:
"Client X experiences pleasant regressions and does things so freely as never before. The client would need this every day."
Therapist:
"Client X is well able to get involved with the strengthening resources of the child and feels the positive transference to the therapist a bit."

The illustrations 4.a-f in the annex (see 4.2) are drawings done by Client B in the course of a therapy (selected out of a total of approx. 30 drawings). Due to space constraints, I refrain from presenting any interpretations. I think, however, that these drawings speak for themselves and show the way of the extension of therapeutic insights, the change of the emotional state and the modification of behavior. The patient was able to reduce his severe dependency on his parents and to enter a partnership for the first time in his life at the end of the therapy.

C) Therapy figures:

Within the framework of his own contributions to the therapeutic work, in a third step each patient is given the task of forming symbolic figures out of clay, wax, plasticine or similar materials to put a shape to important psychic problems.

These sculptures are to be made at decisive points of the therapy, i.e., for example, at the beginning of a therapy, at each point where an important change has been achieved during the therapy, and at the end of the therapy. The patient has to determine himself individually what he wants to represent with a symbolic figure, what is important from his point of view, which type of representation he chooses, and the place where he wants to put his figure on the "therapeutic contact shelf" (the contact shelf is visibly mounted on the wall in the sitting area of the therapy room – see photograph 5 in the annex in 4.2).

The difference to other symbol-specific approaches – for example the approach of Wollschläger and Wollschläger (1998) – is that here non-pre-manufactured objects are used for identification purposes. The task of designing figures personally, of finding a personal form of expressing things allows a broad range of variability and gives the patient the possibility of "comprehending" with his own hands what is symbolically going on internally, and it reveals to me as the therapist what a patient really wants to say when he talks of a deficit, a trauma, a problem, a state, or a constellation.

In the annex in 4.2 you will find photographs of sequences of figures by other patients. The procedure for interpretation during the therapy discussion is comparable to the structure of the three consecutive interpretation levels in connection with the drawings discussed above.

Below I would like to only summarize as an example the general (deliberate) interpretation titles chosen by the patients:

Table 3:

Patient D	1) "The needy little dragon."	At the beginning of the therapy
	2) "Father and son want to play, but can't really get started."	In the course of the therapy (approx. 20th session)
	3) "I take to the road."	In the course of the therapy (approx. 40th session)
Patient E	1) "I pretend to be a witch in order to protect myself."	At the beginning of the therapy
	2) "I live like a nix on the throne, but little viable ashore (in reality)."	In the course of the therapy (approx. 25th session)
	3) "For the first time I feel sheltered in the hammock as back then with my grandparents."	In the course of the therapy (approx. 35th session)
Patient F	1) "I am nailed at my heart to a board like a hunting trophy – without any living emotions."	At the beginning of the therapy
	2) "Full of rage I am stomping on my dead and failing father."	In the course of the therapy (approx. 30th session)
	3) "I rescue my inner child out of the flames and bring him to safety."	In the course of the therapy (approx. 50th session)

I think these examples show both very different and similar paths through a successful psychotherapy of the clients.

There is generally the recognizable tendency to proceed from general, little-differentiated global structures to more and more specific views of a problem. At the end there will then be the sculpture of a person representing an important aspect of the present adult. The patient's commitment to build the figures or to replace them, or any non-appreciation or ignoring of changes will, of course, be a good psychotherapeutic occasion for corresponding analyses of resistances and relationships, since everything is also produced or denied within the framework of these contexts. I find that such information, including the positioning of the figures on the contract shelf (see above), is quite useful and purposeful, and to me they are always a small practical example of the actual status of the therapeutic insights on the part of the patient. Such a procedure yields a certain behaviorally therapeutic benefit which can be an excellent introduction to and accompaniment of the structural, movement therapeutic performances (see case example under 2.1.5).

This independent therapy work will in any case be structural documents for the patients during their difficult self-experience process, on which they may fall back at any time as a reference of their own.

1.3.5 The Approach of Structural Universal Group Therapy

König (2003) describes changes in group-dynamic concepts and practices which today tend to allow for less dynamics and more individuality than previous concepts. That is also the credo of our group work.

The approach of structural universal group psychotherapy was developed by my wife and me during the last three years out of our practice with groups paying for the therapy themselves. They were patients who had done either an approved individual therapy with my wife as a therapist or with me as a treater. During the individual therapies we encountered situations in connection with these patients where a change of the setting in terms of a group work was envisaged as purposeful, because aspects of the family or partnership-related solidarity required the cooperation of several clients or of a therapist couple for the role play performances or the psycho-dramatic performances of problem constellations.

After their participation in a test group (course group), the patients often opted for a closed therapy concept.

As a married couple we have as treaters the advantage that we are both credible and a model for the group with our different female-motherly and male-fatherly views for the structural relationship work. That means for us, of course, also a therapeutic relief in that we are able to work in reciprocal roles – e.g. in a confronting or a supporting way. On the other hand, we can also communicate different perceptions in the group and thus convey a benevolent dissimilarity which is unknown to a majority of the patients. As a group setting we have first the model of the course group, which every interested patient can basically join for orientation purposes.

The second model is the relationship-related more intensive closed group of usually six women and six men whose group capability, after participation in a course group, is evaluated by the therapists perspectively, if the patient is interested to confirm, delay or refuse on appropriate grounds the group indication.

This concept of a closed group is an approach of a more intensive co-operation in respect to the joint disorder diagnostics and of a more effective synergy in respect to the therapeutically new experience. This approach extends to eight therapy meetings within two years. Such group treatments take place on a quarterly basis and cover two and half days at a time with a total of ten double sessions.

An important component of this growth-oriented approach is furthermore the enhancement of the self-help potential. For this reason, at least one small group of the women on the one hand and of the men on the other hand will take place separately between the above-mentioned therapy groups – and at least one large group of all participants without the therapists.

The problem of enhancing the healthiest relationship-dynamic forces in the large and small groups was a point with which we were concerned for quite a long time. At the beginning we were too often confronted with the situation that the joint growth process was counteracted by group members in the "self-help rounds" due to the transference and introjects parts which had not yet been adequately worked on. In addition, the self-organized rounds sometimes left the framework of the therapeutically structured discussion units and group initiatives without any reflection.

Only after a number of experiments were we able to find a good remedy on the basis of the mediator principle, which we usually establish as of the third therapy session and which will then also be extended as a structure to the small and large self-help groups.

The mediator principle is organized as follows: the group of participants, having become familiar with the basic terms of the relationship and group dynamics in the pre-courses, select from their group the female patient and the male patient who at that moment in the group situation represent convincingly the most progressive therapy-related views and who enjoy a certain recognition in the group. The selection of this couple is already from the beginning a dynamic and democratic finding process which has a structurally-clarifying and ego-strengthening effect.

As a result thereof, the subsequent selections will normally be less time-consuming and quite "accurate" in the group with the support of the therapists. In the sexually balanced groups with the same number of female and male patients, each member of the group naturally assumes some leadership and coordination functions within the process of this decision-relation structural development; but the point is that this happens not on a formal basis but on the basis of contents-related rotation principles.

The criteria and particularities of the respective therapy units are coordinated both therapists and mediators right at the beginning of a therapy unit either separately or directly in the presence of the group. Thereafter, the mediator couple sits opposite the therapist couple and control the group process. As responsible therapists we intervene – for a short time – in the group process by correcting or verbalizing things in the case of any complicated misinterpretations or false assessments on the part of the mediators, of any unnoticed infringements of rules on the part of the group members, or any "hidden subjects" which have to be addressed relatively clearly by the "main therapists". Other we have a supervisory function in the group.

By introducing this mediator approach into our structural group work, a new qualitative impetus in the group therapy sequences and the self-help units was made possible. Another positive effect of this approach has been that the problem of working on the resistance during the dependency phase of the group could be significantly reduced. According to the feedback from the patients, the effects of the mediator training in respect to the more adult competences of controlling and structuring of the family and company-related reality of the patients in their external life is to be considered as another advantageous aspect.

In the therapy sequences we work problem-specifically – or facilitated due to these pre-clarifications – less dynamically with "therapeutical working teams" which are established on a project-specific basis for the performance of one of the specified therapy concerns.

At first we generally have a look at the level of the group's capability to work. Should there be any real disorders of relationships, then such disturbances would have priority. Often enough, however, it can be empathetically noted that the transference and introject work are in reality the more powerful background for any symptomatic disorder experiences etc. Then the group needs, "despite all obstacles a cooperatively empathetic "we-feeling", and to that end small group exercise sequences are often developed and carried out within the framework of contact and resource performances. After this stabilization process, the real core work in respect to the performances of each individual group member begins.

In a voluntary sequence of clarity, need, and applicability of the work proposals, the individual concerns are then collected by the mediators and operationalized in a discussion in the group. The group participants, mediators, and therapists pay attention to whether the said concern is comprehensible in this therapy situation and has been adequately derived in terms of its significance. If necessary, possible misgivings or corrective measures are discussed.

If this part of the idea has then been assessed as comprehensible and purposeful after the short "supervision check", and if is considered as quite beneficial or has been corrected accordingly, then the representation of the problem in a performance within the framework of a setting, with the help of symbolizing objects and/or the participants being present (including, of course, the therapists who will also play an active part in the performance) is discussed and decided upon.

When the structure consisting of concerns, objects, and persons has been established, two helpers are chosen. One of the helpers will be the supporter who keeps track of the patient's concern and who may also verbally intervene conducively at the patient's request. The second person selected is the one in whom the patient finds support. This participant pays special attention to the emotional state of the patient carrying out his or her performance. Should the performing patient have an emotional break-down or lose his temper, this helper provides comfort and protection. This supporting process often takes the form of the supporter bringing paper tissues to the exhausted patient, getting him a blanket, providing him or her with physical support after the strenuous performance, and the like.

After completion of the work, these performances are evaluated together in the therapy group, which has returned to the circle of chairs in the meantime, and we try to share any diagnostic and therapeutic perceptions and ideas. When this phase of sharing (Pesso, 1986) and feedback is finished, specific derivations for the patient's everyday life in practice will be worked on within the framework of a creatively yet firmly led discussion in a later integration round. The therapy performances recorded on video can also be worked on later in individual therapy sessions.

1.4 My Own Modifications of a Psycho-Traumatic Approach in Individual and Group Therapy

In this section, I would like to describe which special focuses we set during the practical exercise, and which general procedure we employ when treating well-known or newly-uncovered psychotraumata.

The therapy approaches of Hofmann (1999), Petzold (2000), van der Kolk (2000), Huber (2003 a, b), and Smucker (2003) concurrently point out that a trauma can only be worked on after a phase of psycho-social stabilization. To that end, psycho-educational, rehabilitating, and sometimes drug-specific, as well as administrative, measures are to come first, whereby, of course, the competences of respective institutions and treaters can be used (see authors, ibid.). In certain especially serious cases with multiple traumatizations, this phase can take months or even years.

So the actual traumatological treatment begins with a caring and considerate clarification of the patient's background and the establishment of a respective network, as well as a restriction of any retraumatizing and chronifying influences on the pathology to be treated. Only then will therapeutic enterings into the trauma process be ethically and professionally justifiable. But since the psychotherapist has been allocated little administrative competence, we first try to help the patient with the structural establishment of such a social network. Suitable for this purpose seem to be information materials from public authorities, and information events for patients and their relatives, which we offer within the framework of a small advanced training academy alongside our therapy practice. Furthermore, we include in this set our work with a resource-oriented focus in course groups (see above), where the building of a structure and the establishment of social contacts with others – with both traumatized and/or non-traumatized patients – can be practiced in a non-dynamizing way.

In individual therapy sessions, breathing techniques, expression exercises and perception exercises are used in addition to psycho-educational therapeutic stabilization techniques such as grounding, and practiced mostly for self-application purposes.

In this connection diagnostic and therapeutic methods from Ego States Therapy of Watkins and Watkins (2003) are also successfully applied.

Once this results in the patient feeling safe enough, which the therapist must also verify in their joint therapy sessions or on the basis of the established level of the patient's external behavior competence, we proceed step by step to expose the trauma in the therapy session.

Care must be taken when it comes to the diagnostics of the relationship between the therapist and the patient, as well as to the assessment of the external tasks, since patients tend to easily misjudge themselves and their situations. In connection with some aspects of negative transference, patients will readily minimize any cause for conflicts in order to achieve the desired symptom relief, because, for example, the term "'carrying capacity' of a relationship" is, not yet sufficiently enough understood as the mutually experienced capacity to deal with differences and conflicts. At the same time it necessary that in the course of often three to five trauma therapy sessions, the basic conditions for the temporary psychic destabilization in terms of a generalized trigger are well planned and social securities are adequately established; the "therapist's answering machine as a safety cord" won't be enough in most cases here.

In the case of dissociative disorders it is sometimes necessary, in particular, on the part of the therapist, to verify by means of a very sustainable and sometimes sophisticated interview style whether or not the client is still in contact with the perpetrator (despite earlier assertions) (see references in Huber, 2003 a, b).

The trauma expositions are then carried out specifically according to the specifications of Hofmann (1999, EMDR), Huber (2003 a, b, screening and phase exposition), of Levine (1998, hypno-therapeutic metaphors), of Smucker (2003, Imagery Rescripting and Processing), and of other authors. Thereafter follows the self-created therapy part of the activity-oriented trauma work by means of transitional transference objects.

There are two important reasons for this approach: First, it is typical for trauma patients that they tend to "beseelen" objects both faster and in a more complex way than average neurosis patients do, which is to be attributed to their emotional tendency to regression. For example, while just standing in the therapy room, they are sometimes directly "jumped at associatively" by various objects. Due to this accelerated transference-related ability or the spontaneously experienced labilization, we as therapists also have the possibility of working actively in an activity-oriented (overcoming) way on the trauma process. As an example: By "practicing with a safe distance" to the anxiety-inducing object an important desensibilizing perception and behavior training can be carried out.

Second, we can actively practice corrective traumata resolution actions by means of the objects. The majority of the traumatized patients experiences an intensive feeling of helplessness, of existential threat, and of inferiority in the stressful situation.

For this reason, after the mostly cognitively and psychologically oriented trauma exposition, it is now useful to subsequently also work on and overcome the "shaped behavioral defeat". In particular, in the case of multi-traumatized patients with dissociative disorders we observed that they quickly fell victim again to new traumatizations or could quickly be re-infected by old circles of perpetrators, due to their weakness in establishing boundaries and in self-assertion – even after good trauma expositions. In addition to educational behavioral tricks or organizational safety measures, precisely such activity-oriented subsequent work on the trauma proved to be very efficient (see e.g. 2.1.1.1, 2.1.2.1, 2.1.3.1 u. 2.1.4.1).

In this kind of work the patient learns to confront the frightening object or to oppose the object loudly and directly, to throw things at the object, to hit the object at close range and so on, until the regressive level of anxiety has been mastered well and the patient is able as an adult in the meantime to defend himself or herself against the tormentor in an exemplary way.

This improved self-extraction from the performed threatening situation is often a good indicator of the patient's permanent stability in respect to any retraumatization risks.

Based on the assumption that "transfer resolutions" can also have an alternating effect, similar to the effect of "transfer triggers", we then go on to extend this solution-oriented work-related performance to other model situations with self-selected trial resolution training involving therapeutic object constellations.

Foreign aggressive behavior competences can, for example, be beneficial to overcome a general victim trance. In addition, posed liberation scenes and performed relief actions for the sake of "new children who are to be rescued" have, in many cases and especially in the case of dissociative disorders, a very EGO-strengthening, and in terms of transfer formation, a general effect.

For this part of the treatment, group work often seems to be the obvious choice, because "many birds can be killed with one stone". Such a community offers the possibility of social contacts which in the case of fixed group structures will quickly be superior to a usual group of acquaintances because of the deeper understanding of the symptoms which develops in the course of growing self-experience.

Another point is that the group practices the self-help potential (see above) and will, in the absence of the therapist, be the individual client's first contact partner with regard to support, protection, and organizational structure. Any difficult relationship conflicts will, however, always be bound to the presence of the therapists, who can also deal in detail with the individual in the group.

Furthermore, these therapeutic rounds will also benefit from an improved learning milieu which will be provided by the group, because traumata are worked on in an activity-oriented way (see above) in which the individual members of the group can be available to each other as models, supporters etc.

In addition, this framework provides the opportunity for transfer-oriented trial actions as an intimate team which almost always contributes to spur on the courageous activity of the participant and helps to train solidarity.

The last part of trauma psychotherapy with multi-traumatized clients within the framework of individual and group therapy is then a further reality-related change of relationships and of the behavior in the form of role plays and group discussions in respect to the mastering of everyday life and a further integration into the patient's real, immediate environment. In role play situations we practice in a communicative way, for example, how to master victim-perpetrator dialogues using verbal know-how, and how to stand up to the intellectually intentional confusion caused by the perpetrators, the subliminal threats hidden in subordinate clauses, or the insidious se-ductions in offers. The client learns to determine and control to some extent the structure of the previously feared discussion.

The total strategy of a prophylactic trauma therapy includes that perpe-trator introject interrogations or introject transference role plays can also be done during the advanced role play setting, in order to be able to make vis-ible the inner-psychic dynamics of self-regulation which has been damaged by a trauma or which has been susceptible to a trauma. In this connection, a mixed group of participants with a varying degree of traumatization and other forms of neurotic disorders will also have a catalyzing effect in terms of shorter work on the trauma psychotherapy both in advance and subse-quently. The explicit trauma exposition will, however, still be reserved to the individual psychotherapeutic session in order to avoid that group par-ticipants who are not involved (but also susceptible to disorders) are not un-necessarily burdened with any specific trauma material or that the exposition of traumata is not triggered in an uncontrolled way.

The following scheme (Table 4, next page) might be helpful to better il-lustrate the structured approach in the psychotherapy of multi-traumatized patients. The phases are listed so that they build upon each other. If a phase category cannot be positively filled, the therapy will stagnate or must be postponed at present. And a therapy phase will be skipped, if it is considered superfluous.

1.5 Presentation of My Own Evaluation Concept in the Walk-In Practice of Individual and Group Therapy

The lack of any evaluation of the efficiency of psychotherapy has been criti-cized repeatedly for years (see Schulte, 1993; Grawe, Donati, Bernauer, 1994; Koeme-da-Lutz et.al., 2003, among others).

Since the time of the health-specific political successes of Dührssen's Berlin Studies in the 1960s in Germany (see Dührssen, 1962; Dührssen, Jor-swieck, 1965), however, along with the ethical quality assurance which has also been requested by the above-mentioned authors, the sociopolitical ben-efit of evaluation studies can no longer be rejected.

In the broad application range of body psychotherapy it is in my opinion furthermore absolutely essential that efficiency studies be designed in such a way that the specific limits of the application and indication of a therapeutic method become visible, so that patients can get comprehensive information on such issues as the short-term and long-term strategy of a treatment as well as on both the selectively symptomatic and the complexly symptomatic ef-

Table 4: Treatment scheme of a structural trauma psychotherapy

The therapy phase is distinguished by:	A	B	C	D	E
1. Inventory / stabilization	XXX	XXX			
2. Psycho-education / stabilization	XX	XXX		X	
3. Strengths of self-stabilization resources	X	XXX		XX	X
4. Verification of therapy capability (Indication? Motivation? Contact with the perpetrator?)	XXX	XXX			
5. Practicing of stabilization and recall techniques		XXX		X	
6. Work on less serious anxiety and trauma material		XXX		XXX	XX
7. Trauma exposition (central subjects)		XXX		X	X
8. Activity-oriented work on the trauma or working subsequently on the trauma		XX	XX	XX	XX
9. Activity-oriented behavior transfer exercises, inner trauma prophylaxis		XX	XXX	X	XXX
10. Role play training to deal with endangering persons		X	XXX		X
11. Role play of everyday behavior situations / social integration of therapy successes	X	X	XXX		
12. External trauma prophylaxis by further restructuring of the old and integration of a new social network	XX	X	XX		
13. Detachment phase	X	X	X		

X – *of high importance*
XX – *of very high importance*
XXX – *of extremely high importance*
A   *Involvement of external institutions and cooperation with other experts*
B   Ind*ividual psychotherapy*
C   *Group psychotherapy*
D   Use *of therapy objects as contact media*
E   *Use of stronger transitional transference objects*

fects of a psychotherapy. Only the informed patient will consciously be able to opt consciously for a therapy target and its risks (see Märtens and Petzold, 2002) – only the informed colleague can initiate referrals which will be appropriate in terms of the indication.

Apart from that I consider evaluation measurements up to the catamnesis as a "practical supervision feedback" of any psychotherapeutic work.

In the walk-in practice it is, however, difficult and time-consuming in view of the health insurance programs which proscribe an exact number of minutes for everything, to find appropriate and economically justified measuring instruments for changes and to apply them without having a research crew at hand.

During this first step I have been concentrating my examinations fully on the improved reflection and assessment capacity of long-term treated patients. In this connection, I know, of course, that also external evaluations on the part of the family, environment and, work environment of the client would be valuable criteria for the success. Given the present status of the diagnostic procedures offered, there is, however, the question of who would then examine the respective health criteria of the corresponding reference families, the specific environment, and the respective places of work? An additional assessment problem is also the patient's pre-therapeutic and post-therapeutic reference point in respect to a treatment situation. If the patient's development is below average, for example, can this result then also be a test-related maximum achievable score-specific effect? Beyond this, would it not be more important to measure the potential of the change than measuring any mere initial status (see Guthke, 1996)? Since some analyst colleagues are further of the opinion that a patient would not want to "directly admit" any treatment-related success to the treater anyway, due to the transference problems which are difficult to overcome, because this would be the sign of a completely matured personality, measurement of the therapeutic success gets completely dropped right away by many.

Test procedures do brilliantly at best in connection with psycho-diagnostics of intelligence and property structures, as brain-organic screening tests or predicators for later developmental paths (see Arnold, Eysenck, Meili, 1993, p. 2288 – 2306).

With this first evaluation approach I am only striving for relatively simple quantitative and qualitative comparisons. On the one hand, my wife and I have used the BSI questionnaire (Brief Symptom Inventory) in the version issued by Franke (2000; a brief version of the SCL-90-R questionnaire – see also Hessel, Schumacher, Geyer, Bähler, 2001). This symptom check list serves as a questionnaire at the beginning when a patient registers for a psychotherapy; then after a waiting period of about half a year as a repetition questionnaire when the patient begins his or her therapy (control group measurement), as well as after having been in our in-depth-psychological analytical psychotherapy with a structural universal orientation for at least two years (about 100 or up to 200 sessions; these subgroups were also differentiated with regard to a trauma, an individual, and a group therapy orientation, etc.). This examination will also be continued soon as a catamnesis survey.

What was important in the BSI comparisons – as well as for the above-mentioned authors – were the average changes of the total values and of the profiles of possible complaints.

In addition to this standardized procedure, LEBI (Leipzig Event and Stress Inventory) developed by Richter and Guthke (1996) as well as the STEP questionnaire developed by Krampen (2002) are still in a trial phase; we are not yet in a position to present any results here because the trial samples were too small. The LEBI inventory of the above-mentioned authors has, in my opinion, the advantage that it helps to make the importance of any qualitative life events measurable and also tries to record any change of value-related hierarchies. In contrast, the STEP procedure offers in my opinion the advantage that the current evaluation of patient and therapist are recorded on a graduated basis for one and the same therapy session and can be related to each other – relatively independent of the therapy procedure applied.

On the other hand, I have developed my own survey questionnaire in recent years, specifically tailored to my own research questions. This questionnaire regarding the patient's satisfaction in respect to various social perspectives has not yet been standardized. It makes it possible, however, to show basic distributions of frequencies as they can be represented according to Lienert (1969), Clauß and Ebner (1974), as well as Lohse, Ludwig, and Röhr (1986). Of course, the problem of the validation of the items and of a methodical graduation has not yet been solved this way.

I found it interesting, however, for client groups which I wanted to investigate, to see in which social areas the patients experienced changes to what subjective extent, which transitional transference objects were experienced as especially helpful, and which unforgettable therapy situations in a positive or a negative sense the patients remember (see also Heisterkamp, 1999, in this connection). The frequency with which the patients visit a doctor before or after their psychotherapy are to be compared on the basis of this simple statistical analysis.

2 Practice of Structural Activity-Specific Performances With Symbolizing Objects

2.1 Case Examples of the Use of Objects in Individual Therapy

A positive progression of a structural activity-specific performance including the use of symbolizing objects was described above in 1.3.1 from the *externally perceptible point of view of the therapist*. Now I would like to describe some important extracts from individual therapy sessions as well as some detailed interaction sequences *from the perspective of the therapist's inner reflections*.

In this connection I am going to work out precisely certain key points of the therapeutic decision-making process with respect to leading, accompanying, and following the patients. I will refrain from presenting any direct quotations due to space constraints. I will also refrain from presenting a detailed description of the anamnesis and the respective family-related contexts. A reference to the context will only be provided by the introject transference table and some comments with regard to the development of the therapy so far.

Apart from that, the *case vignettes* concentrate *fully on the current therapy situation* in order to illustrate clearly the specific procedure and treatment strategy. I feel anyway that an interested colleague might later benefit more if he or she has a look at specific case examples by watching the respectively derived video extracts of therapy sessions, because only this way will he or she be able to really grasp many of the vaguely associatively and emotionally laden impressions. But what is not visible in the video, however, are exactly these therapeutic perceptions and conclusions in the mind of the treater.

The list of the case examples from 2.1.1 to 2.1.5 corresponds with the general hierarchical sequence of the therapy phases and the degrees of difficulty in structural universal psychotherapy with activity-specific performances. Methodically I ask myself the following questions in the course of a therapy session:

The therapist's inner self-questioning scheme:

1) What do I know at the moment about the background of the disorder and the target of the treatment agreement?
2) With which concern does the patient open the current session? Which

relationship are we based on here (also independently from the spoken text)?

3) Are there any perception-related deficits or perception-related resistances in the relationship which must first be made conscious or which must be demonstrated by means of therapy objects or exercises?

4) Is there any basic agreement between the patient and the therapist regarding the subject to be worked on or is there any perceptible (suitable) working climate?

5) Towards what aim and with which therapy objects or means could we get a perception- and/or activity-oriented performance going? What do the patient's ideas and reasons look like to that end – what are my ideas and reasons?

6) Which verbalization work, break-off criteria, and solution aids will be required on my part during my participation in the therapeutic interaction process?

7) How can the presently achieved result be verified directly or symbolically?

8) Which consequences will the result have with respect to minor/larger modification steps outside of the therapy (derive any tasks)?

9) How do other life contexts match this solution (to be recorded for follow-up discussion)?

10) Will the patient be able to go home/to work in this emotional state after the therapy session (disaster-specific rules)?

These are the questions I have to deal with in my mind as stage direction criteria during the verbal and activity-specific dialogues. Depending on the perceived resistance or progress, I will thus be either forced or willing, according to my mutually agreed upon duty, to give either a critical or stimulating feedback or to engage myself as favorably as possible. Most of the impressions can still be discussed in more detail later in the follow-up discussions. The ratio between activity-oriented units and psychotherapeutic preparatory discussions or follow-up discussions is approx. 1 : 3.

2.1.1 Case Example of Establishing Contact and of Changing the Setting in Therapy

As described in the theoretical part above, before any body movement therapeutic change of the setting, the patient has to first be made familiar with the basic theory of all terms such as symptom-related regression and shared (mutal relationship-based) regression, transference and countertransference, introject, trauma, stabilization, and disaster-specific plan.

Prior to the first movement in the room or the first activity with therapy objects in each case comes the explanation of the purpose and possible benefit of such an activity-specific diagnostics and therapy. I sometimes also describe small case vignettes which illustrate the procedure.

If the patient agrees in principle to learn something – at first unconscious – about transferences and introjects by means of interaction analyses and to call something of unconsciously hidden or blocked events and of unconscious conflicts to memory, and to retrace any emotions relating to such events and conflicts, then the joint activity-oriented therapy work can begin.

Each process of getting to know one another between individuals and every use of objects begins with contact and trial. The same applies here. That means that I always use bodily movement performances and a contact-specific interaction if I don't yet know so much about a client and/or think that the *practical terms* of transference and introject should first be made conscious by modulations, be descriptively checked, and be explored in the direction they will therapeutically be worked on.

Case Example Sven Reimann *:

Mr. R. is about 40 years old, a freelancer, and unmarried. When he came to me, he wanted explicitly to try for the first time an analytically oriented psychotherapy approach after he had been trying in vain already for about 10 years to treat his narcissistic symptoms with esoterically shaped self-experience-oriented workshops.

For more than 30 sessions at the beginning we had quite a hard time to establish a general psychotherapeutic treatment concept in specific detail because all possible "interesting previous experiences" interfered with the structural makeup. His transference introject chart looked as follows:

Table 5:

	Transference	Introject
Mother	I can't trust women because of their constantly changing/shifting moods.	I feel incapable and uncertain when it comes to making decisions.
Father	I continually feel oppressed and humiliated by other men because theytake advantage of my inferior status.	I can't apologize for making mistakes and find it hard to change course after I've made up my mind.

* Names of this and all other patients have been changed

During the first sessions, which were heavily shaped by relationship-specific resistances, I did only a few contact exercises in order to demonstrate practically – always within the relationship-specific variability of the setting – the actual effects of transferences and countertransferences. Especially effective in this connection was once throwing a bag (yellow bag, see appendix) in a very aggressive, messed-up relationship atmosphere.

In the psychotherapeutic discussion part of the session it was clear right at the beginning that here – as already in some sessions before – only the rational insight was still reality-related. We were both aware of the fact that Mr. R. was actually absolutely furious with his father, and that I, in the countertransference, was absolutely furious with patient's stubborn, endlessly provoking communication style which also reminded me consciously of some self-experience backgrounds of my own.

It was clear, however, that we wouldn't get anywhere for the time being, if we couldn't succeed in making some relationship-specific progress that would improve our joint ability to work and would let me get out of the "target role". No verbal psychotherapeutic work was possible under these circumstances due to the strongly negative contact offer.

At this moment I suggested that we could "continue" our never-ending "concept-related argument" with this yellow punching bag instead of with words, a length of 5 meters as a minimum distance between us, so that we both had our territories with boundaries (marking line with therapy objects).

I explained that the yellow bag would now be the symbol for fierce arguments which we could cast at each other's feet or blame each other – from a safe distance of 5 meters. Each of us would have to provide his own protection and to defend himself independently against the approaching bag. We could each throw our "bag of arguments" as fiercely as we liked. The exercise would end after a maximum of 10 minutes, and then we would talk about what we had experienced, felt, and imagined.

Then we let the attacks take their course, and to be sure, we "didn't pull any punches". Each of us aimed carefully and threw the bag with our full strength – but without any „mad blind fury" which would have otherwise caused me to break off the exercise, since any self-observation capacity vanishes in such cases and any psychotherapeutic evaluation would be absolutely superfluous.

So, we got down to business very directly and threw the bag at each other. After about 5 minutes I noticed that the client no longer threw the bag so hard and not as directly at my head. He seemed to be a bit confused and almost sad. After another three minutes he asked if the 10 minutes were already up, which I answered in the negative. However, I said that we could also stop earlier if any important emotions had emerged and were in progress. He was glad to stop immediately. We opened the windows and sat down on our chairs, exhausted (and a bit covered with sweat).

After a few moments the patient said that he now really no longer felt any rage and was instead sad. He said he was amazed that there been still another emotion in the background, and he thought that he understood that he had the feeling that he was not taken really seriously by anybody. Now he wouldn't "enjoy" aggressions any more. He was also surprised that we had employed our full strength – without anyone going crazy. He knows only situations where rage went off the rails, escalating increasingly until one party was done in.

What followed then were still some explanations and ideas with respect to such attacks of aggression on the part of his father which the patient had psychically experienced as destructive. At the end of the session, he said something else in the sense that it had touched him that I as a therapist wouldn't dodge (in a slang metaphor of his native dialect).

Therapeutic Outlook for the Case Example Sven Reimann:
After this exchange of blows, very good therapeutic work was possible for a longer period of time. It was also much easier for me to understand his aggressive provocations. The patient built a new therapy sculpture consisting of two persons made out of clay which represented two individuals standing (somewhat helplessly) opposite each other with a hand stretched out. Additionally, he reported that at work he no longer felt so reproached by interested customers and that he was more composed when he was confronted with any negative business replies. He had begun to exchange e-mails again with an old girl-friend "just so". Of course, there were still some aggressive arguments afterwards, but somewhat more moderate and so far without any "repeated bag-throwing" as a collusive relief.

Therapeutic Summary of Case Example Sven Reimannn:
Due to massive negative transference and countertransference emotions, hardly any verbal psychotherapeutic work was feasible here. The insights regarding the general transference and introject brought hardly any perceptible relationship- or change-related benefit.

Therefore I decided to enact this destructive contact atmosphere by means of the symbolizing object of the "yellow bag" in a bodily confrontation in order to perhaps open up the possibility of a certain relief of the unproductive tension in the activity-specific process on the spot – accompanied at the same time by a conscious observation of the activities. With regard to the structure of the setting, I decided to choose a confrontative-mutual structure in view of the heaviness of the therapist-bound transference so that the patient could get the feeling of being taken seriously and did not feel humiliated and discriminated.

During the exchange of blows the yellow bag temporarily became the negative transference object which was able to transport the rage between us. During this performance we, the patient and I as the therapist, were both able to act out the patient's negative transference and the therapist's negative countertransference to an extent that was both individually suitable and beneficial for us. After this bodily-enacted symbolic showdown, the working atmosphere became qualitatively significantly better within a relatively short period of time.

Another result was, that due to this actively grown closeness, an underlying analysis subject of the patient became visible which we wouldn't perhaps have detected – or not so quickly – *if the aggressive resistance cover had not been taken away*.

This case example of establishing a contact demonstrates the specific analytical moment and the reason for changing from the verbal to the activity-specific setting. Of course, also at later times during the therapy there will again be contact experiments, especially, if we are confronted again with any changed (unclear) relationship situations, or if the patients dare to make the transition to a group therapy. But here the patients will then normally already select the setting independently.

2.1.1.1 Case Example of Establishing Contact and of Changing the Setting in Therapy

In the case of traumatized patients the general hierarchically sequence of steps of therapy planning is similar to the above procedure; although more time and more sure instinct will usually be required here for coordinating and carrying out the therapy interventions. Since traumatized patients – decompensate more quickly in case of any relationship-related tensions or are retraumatized more quickly in emotionally confusing situations, a benevolent relationship diagnostics is always the first step and the prerequisite of any therapeutic cooperation.

Traumatized patients are often more sensitive with regard to non-empathetic relationship constellations and for them it is necessary to experience more direct support.

Furthermore, they can be triggered more quickly in the body therapeutic movement room by previously unknown (that means not agreed-upon) experiences or therapy objects during activity-specific performances, so that a higher degree of empirical flexibility on the part of the therapist and his or her well-trained observation experience is required.

Case Example Undine Beier *:
Mrs. B. is about 52 years old, jobless, and married. Her father committed suicide shortly before her birth. She grew up in a large family with her mother, stepfather (about 16 years older than her mother), sister (10 years older than the patient), and her sister's husband, and experienced all persons as exerting a lot of influence on her upbringing.

Her transference introject chart looked as follows:

Table 6:

	Transference	Introject
Mother	I am not important, because others can't enjoy me.	I carry out all tasks - as a duty, without consideration of any feelings.
Stepfather	I am only important if I comply with the other's need of support.	I am rather passive in case of any conflicts and can only react.
Big sister	I am loved if I do something to earn it.	If I feel confronted with excessive demands, I just break off a relationship.
Brother-in-law	I am not so valuable as a girl, because women are inadequate.	Anyone who doesn't belong to the family is immediately an inferior human being to me.

This patient, Mrs. B., came to me looking for a treatment because a trauma therapy which had failed. She suffered from the death of her daughter which she had not yet come to terms with, and which existed to a certain extent as an interference background in addition to the depressive neurotic symptoms. This additional layer of symptoms relating to the accidental death of her child had led to a post-traumatic stress disorder. As a result of this post-traumatic stress disorder the patient continuously experienced accident-related images of her daughter as intrusions and constantly imaged fantasy dialogues, so she retreated almost completely from life and avoided any new contacts almost phobically. The trauma therapy carried out by a therapist on the basis of the EMDR procedure before had failed, because she, the therapist, shrank back from the patient's strong emotions and broke off the therapy before it had been finished. The subsequent conversational therapeutic approach didn't yield any success either.

When Mrs. B. came to me looking for a treatment, she noticed immediately the "black bag" (see appendix 4.1) in the large movement therapy room, which she thought was just "terrible". I had the impression that her behavior was somewhat phobic and that her feelings of grief were triggered, because she reported later that she had dreamed again more often of the accident due to the "horrible sight" of the bag.

During the first 25 therapy sessions we prepared the transference introject chart as well as the trauma map with the patient's most important stressful events in terms of a therapeutic approach.

Prior to a repeated EMDR or screening procedure I as the therapist wanted to invite Mrs. B. to first do some easy contact exercises, so that our work and relationship abilities would be adequately tested and improved. Since she had responded so aversely to the black bag in the movement therapy room, I suggested to her that based on a skilful establishing of contact with this object – during which she would be allowed to make use of my help – this sensitive "Beseelen" could be used to organize an anxiety reduction and later a therapy for herself.

Mrs. B. said that the sight of this object was so horrible, disgusting, and nasty that she didn't even want to look at it calmly. I asked her encouragingly what we could do to change something of the appearance of the bag so that this difficult emotion would be reduced. After a short moment, the patient suggested that it could be covered. I let her select an appropriate colored blanket out of the pile of blankets. She took a light-brown blanket and spread it completely over the bag. While doing so, a little smile appeared on her face which I commented on appreciatively.

After another little while I asked her whether a minimal contact with the bag would be possible for her, but she refused. Then I asked her whether I could do something – *in place of her* – in order to weaken the vaguely associatively and emotionally laden impression of the bag. Mrs. B. looked sceptically at me and asked whether I could push it away. Readily I went to the bag and pushed it once around in a circle. Then I asked her whether she didn't want to help *me*. She hesitated again a bit – but was now already more relaxed in terms of her body expression.

She thought that it wouldn't be so good to put her hands directly on the bag today. So I asked her which aid one could use to push the bag while keeping a certain distance. Mrs. B. looked around and decided to take the club (see appendix 4.1). Then we pushed the covered black bag around in a circle together: I did so with my hands, she by means of the "club pusher". Suddenly, we found it fun and amusing so that we made jokes about it ("Like in mining with a coal lorry" and the like).

After an evaluative conversational session we could already push the bag around in a circle without any blanket, and she dared to contact the terrifying object with the club – I was supposed to kick the bag once with my feet, and later she was also able to do this by herself during a resource-oriented work (see below).

Therapeutic Outlook for the Case Example Undine Beier:
After the movement performances Mrs. B. became increasingly more relaxed and anxiety-free in the therapy encounters. She experienced me as a helpful therapist (positive transference development) and within about ten therapy sessions re-gained confidence in a trauma exposition by means of the EMDR procedure, (see below) which we successfully completed within three full sessions. Instead of the previous traumatic images there appeared now, however, new images relating to anxiety and loneliness, which had previously been repressed.

Therapeutic Summary of the Case Example Undine Beier:
Due to the avoiding-fearful (phobic) and triggered traumatically "beseelten" emotional experience of the patient, no further therapy progress was achievable on the verbal level on a short-term basis.

Since the patient experienced little confidence in the therapist, repeated trauma expositions did not seem to be indicated. The first steps of establishing a practically experienceable relationship were therefore made by means of a contact bridge demonstrating solidarity to establish a positive transference.

According to my perception it was necessary that the patient first had first a positive parent transference with the specific therapist, since we would otherwise have risked that the new therapeutic contact might again have a retraumatizing effect, because the previous therapy attempt with a colleague had already failed.

In view of this special negative transference expectation and the patient's strong experience of vaguely associatively and emotionally laden impressions, I decided to break down any contact-related anxieties into small and very small steps. As a therapist I then assumed the model role of a parent towards a fearful child and so to some extent also entered into the negative transference with respect to the feared object, which in this "beseelten" experience was a transitional transference object for the incomplete grief and the mother's latent (imagined) sense of guilt with regard to her daughter's death, as she later stated as a hypothesis.

In our joint discussion later we succeeded in working out the interpretation that we, in cooperation, had pushed away the unjustified guilt a bit and had actively come into contact with the pile of grief. Furthermore, some of the "rigidified endless grief" had come into a state of flux again due to the spontaneous fun, which had been avoided up to that point with helpless anxiety.

In my countertransference it was relatively easily possible for me to sympathize with the patient and to help her to work on the extensive grief in this activity-specific form, which might not necessarily have been possible in the case of a chronic depressive conversational dialogue.

What was important is that the patient herself had addressed the traumatized symptoms so that the success could also be interpreted by her. Due to her practical demonstration, the tested positive therapeutic relationship was the starting point for the later trauma exposition and the neurosis-specific psychological subsequent treatment during which the patient could demonstrate a growing self-initiative.

2.1.2 Case Example of Strengthening Resources in the Introductory Phase of Therapy

In reading the above example cases carefully, you will note that in addition to the contact being opened, they illustrate also that right away a resource strengthening effect is achieved. The benevolent form of establishing a contact in joint movement is a critical positive pre-experience between patient and therapist for the difficult therapy steps. I now explicitly want to give you some examples of strengthening resources within the framework of a body-oriented mutual relationship-based therapy; this constructive stage has ultimately the same purpose.

The phase of strengthening resources and of working with elements to some extent during the structural activity-specific performance work is in my opinion always indicated if I don't know a client yet and want to verify how strong and reliable the client's self-healing powers are, and how cooperatively the client works in the relationship to me, and how the client engages in body movement therapeutically. This phase is also indicated if the patient declares that before dealing with a difficult therapy focus, he or she requires a transitional phase of stabilization so that a healthy hope for success can be established.

Extended Case Example of Sven Reimann *:*
Mr. R., who was already described above in terms of his social and neuro-

sis-related structure (see 2.1.1 above), was in about the 45th session in a very soft relationship phase in which he was looking for support. In preparation for this session he had made a drawing of a little boy in a treetop lying there as in a bird's nest and playing with a spotted woodpecker. During the psychotherapeutic conversational part we collect interpretations according to the concept described under 1.3.4 (see above). In this context we found out that Mr. R. had longed since boyhood for a separate space, which he didn't have in his large family with five siblings. In his therapeutic interpretation he thought that in his case it would probably always tend to be a basic acceptance rather than a wish and the general experience of loneliness in the large family; at the moment he believed, however, that the shame of the misery was still strong and that he could not allow himself to get sadder, because he had just assumed an "important task" at his job that didn't "allow any such exhausting work".

He had actually been looking forward to the session, he told me, and he would rather have encouragement, etc. So I decided to refrain that day from working analytically on the resistance, because I could understand "both inner sides" and also knew about his current existential dreads as a freelancing course leader. In addition, I thought that important psychotherapeutic aspects had been identified correctly and would also basically "mature by themselves", if the direction of the relationship in terms of our work was the right one. Maintaining the positive transference wishes was at that moment another developmentally enhancing aspect which could also be supported by an appropriate performance.

So I informed Mr. R. about my ideas, and then we created a setting closely derived from his drawing or his daydream fantasy: We selected the therapy egg as a closed nest in a tree and put it up as a kind of igloo with an open entrance. Mr. R. decided to take blankets, pillows, a penguin as a spotted woodpecker substitute, and a little lion as his friend in the form of a stuffed animal with him into the round ball nest.

He wanted to stay in contact with me via a small rope which he asked to wind slightly taut around my arm; he put the other end of the rope under his pillow and laid himself into the cave nest while staying in visual contact with me. He smiled, satisfied like a child, and closed his eyes. After a few seconds he opened his eyes again and looked at his little lion. Then he began spontaneously to speak for the lion and said with a somewhat articificial child's voice to the penguin that it could come in. Using his other hand for the penguin in the game, Mr. R. let the penguin answer with another child's voice that it never before had been in a lion's cave and that it would be a bit afraid. The little lion laughed and said in terms of a somewhat modified proverbial saying: "What the little lion isn't acquainted with, it won't eat." As a observer I couldn't help but laugh about this funny creative dialogue, and so we were both somewhat happy to see how the other one was laughing heartily.

After a brief pause, the patient said that the nest would now be a bit too narrow for him and that he would come out of it. After another little while we asked each other almost simultaneously what we could still do with the remaining approx. eight minutes. If even a lion could be a penguin's friend, then a peaceful encounter might actually also still be possible here.

The idea which caught our eyes was the holding rocker, because there was still our contact rope lying on the ground. Thus we took the holding rocker, got into the closed rope, and then, while standing at an angle in the rope, we let our bodies fall to the outside in a finely attuned way. The holding rocker was perfectly safe today (as expected). Once we had enjoyed this enough, the client suggested that we might sit down on the floor again. When we did so, I noticed that our feet were only a few centimetres apart from each other. So I asked whether we should not try a touching contact with out feet; the patient found that the idea was great. After a few interested and also a bit funny feet contacts the session was over.

Therapeutic Outlook for the Expanded Case Example Sven Reimann:
After this resource-oriented analytic body therapy session, the patient was for the first time kind of high spirits for a longer period of time. He fulfilled his work-related duties satisfactorily, and his preparations for the therapy became more extravagant and better with regard to the contents. Altogether, he now revealed a broader range of behavior in his individual therapy as well as in his private life, and he experienced his narcissistic needs being nourished. In the conversation we had subsequently, the patient understood that his parents had not been able or hadn't wanted to give him the opportunity of being creative and of having fun, and that he was now feeling increasingly strong enough "to collect the abandoned boy soon".

Therapeutic Summary of the Extended Case Example Sven Reimann:
Due to the previous experiences I had had that day with Mr. R., I opted for a resource-strengthening performance, because any confrontative procedures might – in connection with a relatively good relationship climate – have provoked again the old transference-related weaknesses in him. The therapy egg was an superbly suitable symbolizing object for the nest and was therefore able to transmit the positive, protective relationship atmosphere.

The little play with the penguin and lion reflected something of our specific closeness and of our anxieties. Based on the play the patient was able by working symbolically with these transitional transference objects to dare to make the next direct step in the relationship, which he had already anticipated and outlined for us by his spontaneous dialogue.

We began the holing rocker exercise again in a more adult upright posture at a certain distance, which was made possible by the transferring object of the holding rocker. The allegory of the holding rocker was the metaphor that in a therapeutic regression both sides must equally (mutually) engage in the regression experience so that the relationship can maintain its "durability" and "carrying capacity". If one of two in the holding rocker just wants to stand there (stiffly) or just wants to lean back (egoistically) and to hang in it, then the balance of the holding rocker (the balance in the relationship will topple (see photograph of the holding rocker in the appendix under 4.1).

The positive experience here again resulted in a growth of regressive courage for a new experience which became the basis for a new bodily contact experiment as a good relationship experience, the mutual foot contact, which he had never experienced before.

In this activity-oriented performance, the foundations were laid for the patient's resources for later more stressful therapy work, and at the same time small solutions for new relationship experiences were found "quasi by accident".

2.1.2.1 Case Example of Strengthening Resources in the Case of Traumatic Pathology

Similar to the above concern (see under 2.1.1.1), in the case of traumatized patients, the therapy stage of strengthening resources is more important and has to be treated more in detail than in the case of neurotic clients. The actual trauma exposition work is often preceded by a stabilization and resource enhancement phase which may last for months or under certain circumstances for several years (see, Huber 2003, vol. I and II, as well as Hofmann, 1999).

In this section, I would like to come again to the case example of Undine Beier described above (see ibid.), in order to be able to describe the principle of small steps more descriptively:

Second Case Example of Undine Beier*:
Mrs. B. had in the meantime become surer in establishing contact to me and reflexively more competent with respect to her symptoms of the post-traumatic stress disorder described above. She no longer avoided speaking of her grief over the death of her daughter and her irrational feelings of guilt.

In addition, she had also already succeeded in reducing the intrusions of accident-related images a bit. And she had clearly defined the aim that she finally wanted to get rid of these stressful symptoms, something she hadn't stated so clearly before, because the process of recovery had been sustainably impaired by negative transferences and destructive self-introjects. Within the framework of this inner dynamic it was not entirely permissible to give one's own life, without any guilt, a more important meaning than that of the mourning process.

The point of this therapy stage was thus to look for further resources enhancing the self-healing process and positive self-attributions, before the roots of the transferences and introjects could be addressed more directly by a focus-oriented work.

As a therapy object we again used the black "mourning bag" for our joint interactions. After the "pushing without any cover or guard" (see 2.1.1.1) had worked so successfully, the aim was now to achieve some further reductions of anxiety.

In a movement therapeutic session I asked the patient how we might further deprive the terrifying bag of its power? At first the patient only had the idea that we might expand the distance to now approx. 5 meters (from previously 3 meters). From this distance the patient could just manage to still look at the bag without being afraid. Now we thought about possible ways how we might achieve a reduction of her anxiety. Upon my inquiries, Mrs. B. remembered an incident in her childhood where she had once thrown a stone at a nasty dog at a distance, which unexpectedly had then put its tail between its legs and run away.

So we looked for any suitable throwable objects, which we found in the form of balls, rods, and foam rubber pillows. I again had to start throwing at the bag first, then she did so, and finally we both threw at the same time on command.

While attacking the bag, Mrs. B. got nearly two meters nearer to the bag without noticing it and kept throwing things at it vigorously. While doing this, her feelings alternated between rage and to some extent also fun. When reflecting these feelings which I had observed to her, she smiled awkwardly and asked me, how I would interpret this. I answered her that these might possibly all be repressed feelings, which on the one hand belonged to the mourning process but which on the other hand might also have still other connections, but which need not concern us too much at the moment since we would be having subsequent evaluation discussions. At that moment we should think about how we might succeed in reducing the level of anxiety even further.

The patient said that another attack might perhaps be required so that the bag would be defeated once. When I asked her whether she thought of using any intermediate objects or only her hands or only her feet, Mrs. B. decided after a time to use her feet without any additional aids. She had used such a strong kick once before in the school yard when, standing in front of a hostile boy, she had successfully kicked backwards, like a horse does, against his shinbone. I praised this idea of kicking and asked her in which setting we should do the kicking: Individually one after the other, together in one direction, or together against each other with the bag between us? Mrs. B. clearly wanted to kick *together with me backwards in one direction*. So we started. The patient really proved to have much strength in her legs, so that I was hardly a match when I tried to kick simultaneously.

After about three minutes, she suddenly turned around and kicked forward, and then so did I. According to my observation, it was a serious but at the same time also a relatively anxiety-free kicking. After another two or three minutes, she paused for breath and smiled slightly when she saw that I was somewhat exhausted. Then she said, it "can still take something", meaning the bag, went for the clubs and handed one club over to me. I understood without any words what had to be done now, and together we hit "the bag relatively calmly", rhythmically and simultaneously. After a few minutes, it was finally over, and the patient went home in good mood.

Therapeutic Outlook for the Second Example of Undine Beier:
Mrs. B. told me that days later she had still been burning for action. She had cleared out her daughter's wardrobes and put the clothes into collection bags for the Red Cross in order to help needy people in the third world. Suddenly, it had come to her mind that her daughter had previously also given away things very generously, and she believed that this behaviour would have been in accordance with her daughter's wishes. Following additional focus-oriented movement sessions and a repeated trauma exposition on the basis of the EMDR procedure, she cleared her daughter's room and equipped and used it, after it had been renovated, as a hobby room for herself.

Therapeutic Summary of the Second Case Example of Undine Beier:
After the contact exercises, Mrs. B. still showed an avoidance-specific behavior towards the bag as a transitional transference object for many "beseelte" connections such as, for example, the pile of grief, the pain she had experienced, her repressed rage, parts of her dead daughter, and parts of irrational guilt fantasies she experienced, which were all embedded in this object due to her associative "Beseelen". During our later work, it turned out additionally, that the black bag was also a symbol for her dead father and the character weak stepfather. This had, however, not yet been a topic at the time of the

currently described session or of our subsequent conversation. It should be added that there was later also the interpretation that negative transference parts of the patient referring to the therapist had also been "hidden" in the bag the patient had kicked so furiously.

That means the bag had been a multi-functional transitional transference object for the client's perceptible experience parts.

The accompanying mutual relationship-based interaction with the therapist had been an important performance opener, because the phobic and post-traumatized patient would otherwise hardly have gotten into an activity flow within such a short time. When organizing the structure of the settings, the patient's resource experiences had always been activated first and transferred into performance pictures, so that she was able to bring about spirited solutions on the spot.

During the differentiated relationship modulation, Mrs. B. repeatedly expressed at the beginning her need for support; but gradually this changed to a growing self-initiative with competitive tendencies with respect to the therapist (e.g. collecting the clubs and hitting more persistently than the therapist).

Although the focuses of the background of the delayed grief and the interconnectedness of the post-traumatic stress disorder with previous non-resolved stressful events, some of which had been stored as traumatizing, were only treated at a later time, this resource-oriented movement work on an projection-capable object was a good and important preliminary stage for the psychotherapeutic steps that were to follow later.

The psycho-physical strengthening in the movement based on the therapist's mutual relationship-based involvement in connection with the desired support probably made possible later the effective trauma exposition of the intrusion images on the basis of the EMDR procedure.

2.1.3 Case Examples of a Focus-Related Work on Inner-Psychic Problems

In the contact- and resource-oriented movement performances (see 2.1.1 to 2.1.2.1 above), the client should learn to perceive his or her positive and negative transference feelings and to differentiate and modify them in a setting.

The aim of the focus-oriented activity-specific performances is to verify in a next deepening step a central transference and to transport it into a dynamic interaction to work on it, where a first or partial solution of the problem or conflict to be treated will consciously be possible.

Therefore, the patient is asked to add a focus and solution fantasies to the transference introject chart, which had been specified by the patient during the preparatory therapy sessions as his or her "problem which has to be investigated". The therapist then contributes his or her perception to it.

The client's focus is agreed upon between the patient and the therapist, discussed and formulated in the words of the client in order to enhance the independent activity-specific motivation on the part of client as far as possible.

In addition, I outline all terms also *from the therapist's point of view*. Depending on the level of the transference, development, and relationship between the patient and the therapist, these terms may be compatible with the client's terms, have a different emphasis, or may sometimes also be formulated and aligned completely different as a research hypothesis.

When working out the patient's focus, I do this on the basis of the thoughts of Maaz (1997a), who understands the central psychodynamic search hypothesis of the patient as an active working alliance between the treater and the client.

The construction of the therapist's focus is oriented on the analytic principles of Balint (1970) and the further developments of Lachauer (1999), for whom the focus is the central perception hypothesis with regard to the patient's disorder in the therapist's experience, which comprises both the patient's currently conscious disorder problems and the patient's possible unconscious defense backgrounds, as well as any circumvented solution possibilities.

Based on the similarity or dissimilarity between the patient's and the therapist's focuses, I have to draw my conclusions within the framework of my structural approach in terms of certain setting-related requirements, indications, and limits, which I will comment briefly in connection with the case examples below.

Since the aim is now to work increasingly on central points of the disorder, the transference introject chart also has to be extended by the following dimensions: the focus from the therapist's point of view and solution, as well as boundary criteria. According to my previous experience I would like to add that these items should, however, be re-formulated or differently formulated after a few months with respect to the contents.

Case Example of the Patient Felix Müller *:
The patient is about 25 years old, a student of business economics, and unmarried. He came to me with depressive symptoms and sexual compulsory fantasies looking for psychotherapeutic treatment, after he had begun a psychoanalytic treatment and a direction of studies in another university city

and had broken off both because of "inadequate success". The colleague's diagnosis was: Depressive neurosis with a psychosomatic complex of complaints.

Below you will find Mr. Müller's transference introject and psychodynamic work charts:

Table 7:

Transference/Intro-ject on the basis of		Dimension in the Patient's Experience and Behavior	
		Transference	**Introject**
Mother	the patient's point of view	I am afraid to disappoint women, because the withdrawal might otherwise be even stronger.	Mistrust towards people and withdrawals in order to be not vulnerable.
	the therapist's point of view	Supporting women in order to get love in return as a reward.	Egocentric interpretation of conflict causes.
Father	he patient's point of view	Men generate expectation pressure against which I must defend myself.	Compulsory and obstinate behaviors.
	the therapist's point of view	Humiliating and destroying men.	Letting all run their heads into a wall, based on a rational style.
Psychodynamic Work Chart			
Focus	he patient's point of view	I am afraid of strong emotions, because they stress my body and I can't yet believe that opening myself would bring any improvement.	
	the therapist's point of view	I want to open few feelings, because I fear that feelings will destroy, and I can't imagine that emotions will make possible any growth.	
Ways of Solution / Limits	he patient's point of view	• No ideas about a solution. • I would not like to be labilized so much that my studies would be endangered.	
	the therapist's point of view	• Contact perceptions. • Body performance exercises. • Enhancing any positive parent transferences to the therapist. • Reviewing motivation; animating to self-activity	

After Mr. M. again opened a session which had originally been agreed as a body movement session with bodily complaints, I suggested in view of the above psychodynamic work chart that the patient should once try to represent the body scheme he felt by means of the symbol objects available in the room, and then to explain it in hypotheses. I explained that it would be good, if he first put down without any interruption all important body parts in the form of the objects, and if we then talked about the hypotheses with regard to the meaning and function.

As a therapist, I consciously decided to select this relationship form in order not to get too much into a transference interaction, to invite him to initiate activities by himself, and to learn something about his body scheme, which, by the way, has the effect that I as the "learner" get into a positive transference role.

After having looked around for a short time, the patient began to draw the giant egg (see appendix 4.1) on to the giant mat, with the comment that the mat represented the body as a whole and the giant egg the heavily thinking head.

Thereafter, he put a small round pillow under the head that represented the belly, and a larger colored foam rubber pillow for the heart next to it on the left. Then he took the clubs and laid them as arms between the head and the line of the belly and heart down on the floor. Finally, he took two small batacas (foam rubber bats) and laid them as legs unrelated to the rest at the lower side to the body – without any pelvis.

When he said that he had finished, I asked Mr. M. just to look at his body image and see what effect it had on him, and then to explain the functioning of this body to me. To that end, he should go to the respective body part, put his hand on it, and try to talk about the meaning of this body part and, if possible, also the feeling that emerged in him in this connection.

First, the patient went to the head and touched it with a smile. Mr. M. thought that the head was actually the giant central control station that hardly felt anything, but just wanted to observe everything meticulously. Next, he tapped on the belly and added, that then everything which could not always be digested would disappear "here"; therefore he had chosen the round pillow (belly pillow, see appendix 4.1). The heart, Mr. M. then said, would really be such a "soft thing" because it couldn't cope with so many things. The hands (represented by the clubs) served as a defense towards the outside, but were hanging at the moment only limply on the body, as did the legs.

Praising his good perception and symbolization as impressive, I asked him whether he could go a step further and try to assign the location of the centers for certain feelings which I would now list at random. If he thought that a certain feeling was placed nowhere in the body, he could just refuse to allocate this feeling by saying: "Doesn't exist in me!"

First I mentioned the feeling of guilt. Without hesitating, the patient bent over the body and touched the belly (belly pillow). Then I said: fear. The patient hesitated a bit and then touched the heart. In the third place I said: rage. The patient didn't find any body part corresponding to that feeling. When stating the fourth term, inferiority, the patient again touched the foam rubber pillow (colored pillow). The term emptiness as well as the term grief didn't meet with any response. When I dropped the last keyword for the time being, ambivalence, the patient touched the large head (giant egg) again.

As a third structural exercise I asked Mr. M. whether he was prepared to still work on one or two hypothetical solution ideas and try to see whether he had an idea how we might help this tormented body lying in front of us.

At first, the patient seemed to be astonished and asked me to repeat the instruction. Repeating it, I emphasized that "this model body" could or should not lie there so helplessly forever, and that we could just talk shop like two "experts" about the chances of finding a solution. The patient pondered a bit, and then he said, that the club hands could just fend off any reproaches and other attacks. Apart from that, the head would be too large and too hollow, it would have to be "replaced" in favor of stronger feet. As the "expert observer" I found this idea great and gave him a short signal with a gesture to replace the head. The patient took a small gymnastics ball as a head and two pillows as symbols for the feet. I said that this model human being could really stand much better now, and then ended the session since the time was up.

Therapeutic Outlook for the Case Example of Felix Müller:
In the following sessions, Mr. M. was able to talk much more openly and with more motivation about the inner connections between emotions and the body, which he was suddenly observing with interest of his own.

He could logically derive that he repressed, anger and rage, in particular, because he was afraid of their strong impact. We came to an agreement that we should therefore try to experiment "carefully" with aggressiveness in further activity-specific performances. To that end we then selected joint kicking exercises with the bag (in view of the feet which were to be "strengthened") and a joint throwing of the bag (see above, case example of Sven Reimann), which very soon led to a strengthening of the patient's aggressiveness.

Without having been requested to do so, he went through important conflicts with his girl-friend and his father three weeks later, which gave him a basic insight into the "subliminal psychodynamics" of his neurosis with a psychosomatic defense structure. His university performance became more constant in the course of the therapy.

Additional role performances are still going on currently; but the breakdown of the psychic bodily links was a good way to lead up to this point.

Therapeutic Summary of the Case Example of Felix Müller:
Due to the patient's heavy defenses and the resistance in the relationship, I suggested doing a symbolization task with respect to the patient's complaints during the first focus-oriented part of the treatment, because the patient was "kept remaining there" and hadn't offered any psycho-physical connections in the therapy sessions. In practice it became evident that on the *specific activity-related level* of selecting the symbolizing objects a committed action from the patient came into play, which he had never shown before in any psychotherapeutic conversations so far.

He selected relatively strongly expressive objects, which he could roughly "beseelen" with emotional states during the second question round. In my view, this opened the possibility of gaining a cautious insight into his psycho-physical inner structure.

In the context of the self-chosen and self-interpreted symbols, after the easy "Beseelen" of the objects, it was then possible to formulate initial solution approaches to his psychodynamic problem in this object language, which I, as the therapist, supported actively and sympathetically. As a result thereof, the positive transference to the patient was able to grow again a bit, something that had not succeeded earlier in the conflict-oriented conversations.

Due to the creative performance of the arm and leg activities, the jointly worked out focus on the aggressive deficiencies in conflict-laden situations could lead to an "immediate activity-specific active solution" in a joint motion of development. And that was a decisive point from which the patient progressed rather quickly.

Only after I had in practice provided evidence of my positive "inclination to support the client", was Mr. M. able to carry out with me quite normal but important relationship-specific clarifications in the therapy sessions – without relapsing again into a negative father transference.

Case Example of the Patient Anna Daum *:
Mrs. D. is about 28 years old, an employee, and unmarried. She began a therapeutic treatment because she had serious identity problems with herself and in her partnership, complained about depressive crises, and experienced herself in her relationship to her divorced parents as still dependent and in her relationship to her son as still clinging.

Her psychotherapeutic work charts looked as follows:

Table 8:

Transference/Introject on the basis of		Dimension in the Patient's Experience and Behavior	
		Transference	Introject
Mother	the patient's point of view	I have to adapt, otherwise I will lose all affection for a long time.	I am obtrusively aggrieved and am filled with envy towards everything that feels healthier than I do
Mother	the therapist's point of view	I have to support my mother, because I might otherwise be destroyed.	I always want to be the center of attention, because otherwise I don't feel that I exist.
Father	he patient's point of view	I have to take care of the others, because otherwise I will be abandoned coldly.	I belittle others, although I can hardly stand any criticism. the therapist's point of view
Father	the therapist's point of view	I try to please all men, because otherwise they might suddenly take revenge on me.	I depreciate and denounce others in general, because otherwise I can't justify or support my self-esteem.
Psychodynamic Work Chart			
Focus	he patient's point of view	I adapt myself very much to the emotions of others – up to the state of dependency, because I fear otherwise being destroyed by the emotions of others.	
Focus	the therapist's point of view	I strive for the feelings of being accepted and understood by others, up to the point of giving up my identity, because otherwise I will be repelled with my wishes for ever, and because I can't imagine that there is anybody really and truly interested in me.	
Ways of Solution / Limits	he patient's point of view	• Learning to talk without any fear about all facets of emotions. • Giving up the dependency on unloving persons.	
Ways of Solution / Limits	the therapist's point of view	• Supporting any strivings for detachment. • Making visible in the relationship any vulnerability in terms of feeling hurt and disappointments. • Enhancing positive transferences and emotions of true acceptance.	

During a planned body movement therapy session Mrs. D. and I looked for a perception- and activity-specific performance where the focus she had worked out including the problem symptoms and solution fantasies could be set in motion. Finally we thought of a scene with harnesses, because several times during our conversion in this therapy session Mrs. D. had talked of her inability to just go away to and leave her parents standing there with their feelings. She thought that it would be really good for once if she got the feeling of dependency and then could experience becoming significantly stronger and not having to bow to the old obligations and fears any more.

During the activity-specific performance Mrs. D. put on the harnesses (similar to a baby's belt for adults – see appendix 4.1), which I closed with a belt. When I fastened the buckle on her back, I already felt the patient's slight difficulty in breathing (with a relatively loose chest belt), which I perceived to be a sign of the beginning regression.

She looked around a bit fearfully and wanted to set out already, when I stopped her for a moment and pointed out that it would be quite important for an adult personality to know where she wanted to go to: So, what might we symbolically lay in the other corner of the room as an attractive target for orientation purposes? Mrs. D. opted for stuffed animals (a lion, a beaver, a fox, a dog, and a little horse), which she referred to in general as a group of same-age friends – for instance, roommates. Then she leaned herself into the harnesses a bit as if she wanted to set out and asked me, whether I wanted to stop her now.

I told her that I would only do so in order to help her during this exercise, and that we could start now. The patient stamped vigorously in the direction of the stuffed animals. I tried as hard as I could to stop her, so that she really came to a halt after about 3 meters. She looked back to me somewhat furiously, and I encouraged her not to stop and to keep running away from the parents who made her dependent; if necessary, she might also curse in order to support herself and to mobilize more strength. Then the client began to puff and snuffle loudly (like a horse) and to curse something unspecifically ("Damn it!"; "Let me go!"; "Take care of yourselves along!" and the like). After approx. 5 minutes she had finally reached her group of stuffed animals, exhausted but happy. I had mobilized a counterforce of about 80 – 90 %, in order to give her the possibility of experiencing a true struggle – but not again an absolute helplessness or defeat – and a "hard-won true victory".

When the patient left to go home, she was obviously happy and moved.

Therapeutic Outlook for the Case Example of Anna Daum:
Mrs. D. was clearly strengthened after the activity-specific performance. When evaluating the therapy session, she recalled a further number of humiliations and discriminations or unfair treatment she had experienced at the hands of her parents. These incidents had come to her mind as a follow-up to the movement analysis. Her father, in particular, had imposed many feelings of guilt upon the girl because of his unsatisfied moods, and the mother had hinted to her daughter at a possible suicide, if she didn't manage to get along in her marriage. All these burdens had made her dependent as a child, and she told me that she had in many respects gone without playing with peers, etc. because she was compelled "to be worried".

A result of these deeper memories was also that the patient's anger due to the "independence she had missed" grew significantly.

As a consequence, she wrote a letter to her father with which she wanted to clarify their relationship. In this letter she renounced various promises she had given to him earlier. With regard to the mother, she already felt that she had become stronger so that she was ready to talk directly with her. During this conversation, she suggested to her mother to look for a "real psycho-therapy" because nobody could or was obliged to help her with the manifold psychic problems she had.

Therapeutic Summary of the Case Example Anna Daum:
What became obvious in the area of associations in this therapy session on the basis of the inner-psychic problems she had enacted (see work charts) was the focus of the patient's dependency problems to be worked on. Thanks to the activity-specific performance with the harnesses, we managed to vividly demonstrate an inner-psychic situation, which on the one hand corresponded with the previous status of experiences, but which on the other hand confronted the patient with the necessity to find potential solutions for these problems or which helped to provoke "resources enabling her to cut the cord".

In this connection, the aspect of an inadequate objective and of an insufficient solidarization with peers was able to be "quasi incidentally" also included in the performance.

By assuming the stopping function as a therapist within the framework of the conceptual boundaries of the setting, I provided the patient with the opportunity for an external resistance experience, which she hadn't always really consciously experienced or noticed with her real parents (or wasn't allowed to notice due to their defenses). Therefore, I consciously slipped directly into the role of the negative transference for a short time, which at the same time also applied to me as a therapeutic negative transference, and helped the patient to find a behavioral solution, which her real parents hadn't be able to allow so far (in the end, I had not stopped or prevented everything with my full strength). Since the patient was forced to make great efforts, this trial solution was very credible to her. In addition, she could also get a sustainable impression of her real (adult) strength in terms of "setting out bodily", which so far had not been reflected to her by her parents.

The patient could obviously make good use of this trial experience as an opportunity and a inner pre-experience and introduce some important external behavioral changes.

Due to the (real) dependency situation which the patient experienced increasingly more intensively, the harnesses temporarily became transitional transference objects of the disorder she was experiencing.

As a result of this therapeutic help, including the fact that the therapist enabled the patient to find a specific better solution, the originally negative transference situation in the relationship was transformed to a positive parental transference, which we could draw on during our later therapeutic work as a transformation experience.

2.1.3.1 Case Examples of Focus-Related Work on Traumatic Pathology

In structural psychotherapy the aim is on the one hand to concentrate on pathology-specific focuses relating directly to the traumatic material of the experience, and on the other hand to work out disorder-specific focuses representing indirectly the neurotic framework of the traumatic scene or the developmental genesis up to the traumatic performance.

In terms of the treatment it will make a great difference whether we are facing a monotrauma in an otherwise more or less intact relationship atmosphere or whether the trauma is only the peak of a chronically damaging (family-specific) influence. Accordingly, the focuses will have to be put differently, which, of course, will also apply to the relevance of the direct or more indirect activity-specific performances.

Therefore, the first case example describes the focussing including a direct work on the trauma, whereas the second case example shows such a focussing including an indirect work on the trauma.

Case Example of the Patient Franka Schulze *:

Ms. S. is about 25 years old, a student, and unmarried. When she came to me, she was specifically looking for a psychotherapeutic treatment of the sexual abuse she had suffered at the hands of her father between her 10th and 15th year of life. Filled with shame, she had avoided working on this issue in the ensuing years. Faced with nightmares, intrusive stimuli, and sexual experience disorders, she had realized in the meantime that she was unable to deal with these experiences by means of any cognitive formula methods or by simply trying to forget. What additionally aggravated the student's situation on a social level and added a neurotic conflict problem to her reason to seek treatment was the fact that she was struggling with her parents for financial support. The psychodynamic work charts of Ms. S. were as follows:

Table 9:

Transference/Intro-ject on the basis of		Dimension in the Patient's Experience and Behavior	
		Transference	Introject
Mother	the patient's point of view	I adapt myself perfectly, because I believe that I otherwise will not be loved any more.	I disparage and humiliate adults and children without any empathy.
	the therapist's point of view	I can't feel myself without any achievement and perfection, because I don't feel any identity, and I orient myself according to what pleases others.	I rail against others crudely and contemptuously and to weaken them undifferentiatedly.
Father	he patient's point of view	I don't at all feel accepted as a woman, because my personal charisma is inferior	I hate many people and desperately beg other for love, although it is unavailable there.
	the therapist's point of view	As a woman I always believe myself to be at a disadvantage, because I store all critical feedback carefully in my memory.	I hate people or tend to subordinate myself completely to them, because I can only destroy or be dependent.
Psychodynamic Work Chart			
Focus	he patient's point of view	I am striving for adaptation, achievement, and perfection, because I am basically feeling inferior and let others do anything with me. As a compensation, I destroy others with scorn.	
	the therapist's point of view	What distinguishes me are compulsory achievement and adaptation traits, because I can't feel myself in my identity, and therefore I have to get rid of any unpleasant feelings, and because I can't image that there could be any real affection and support for me.	
Ways of Solution / Limits	he patient's point of view	• Studies must be mastered. • I have to be able to get a job. • I want to get rid of the mental pictures of sexual abuse. • I must make myself independent from the entire deformative style of my parents.	
	the therapist's point of view	• Respect the patient's capability. • Prior to the trauma exposition, the patient must have a positive and supporting relationship to the therapist as a parent substitute. • It must be ensured that the patient's narcissistic needs will be filled and nourished in respect to the subjects of loneliness and emptiness, and that a conceptual differentiation of the term betrayal is provided to her.	

In view of the above-mentioned problems, I decided to begin for the time being with contact- and resource-oriented activity-specific performances, as described in the sections (2.1.1 and 2.1.2) above.

The patient responded especially well to the hammock and the children's swing, where I helped the "child" in a fatherly (or rather grandfatherly way) to come to rest, because she often used to talk at breakneck speed in other settings and had tried to associate "analytically-well" in order to please the therapist father and to get a quick approval or affirmation "for everything". What was noteworthy during this swinging in the hammock in calm contact were her quick regressions to the fearful girl with her yearning and fearful children's eyes. She said that she would be dreaming of good parental hugs; in view of the above-mentioned problems and the patient's psychic fragility I affirmed this verbally as very understandable, yet avoided it as an activity-specific part of a performance.

During a scene with stuffed animals and infantile play dialogues, I noted a first cautious approach in terms of a hand contact, which I referred to as a therapeutically nested establishment of contact: With her stuffed animal beaver the patient approached my big brown bear (which had been allocated to me) and wanted to touch it playfully, from stuffed animal to stuffed animal, so to speak. Suddenly, she shrunk back fearfully and said that it was still too early to do this and that she needed the help of the hedgehog, which she spontaneously took out of the animal box as a bridge figure. Then her beaver touched the hedgehog, and the hedgehog was able to or was allowed to touch the brown bear. Now, the child in her shone as brightly as a sun. At the end of the session, Ms. S., well-progressed again, asked whether she could take the hedgehog home with her once "because of its good help", and I allowed her to do so.

A few days later, the client bought herself a stuffed animal bird, which looked a bit funny and would always rescue the child, whenever it needed help. Therefore, the hedgehog was returned to me with thanks.

When during a stabilizing swinging in the hammock, Ms. S. then really wanted to touch my hand and was able to endure everything well, we had found through the verbal evaluation a criteria which suggested that the trauma exposition could begin now in a closer sense. The patient had learned to consciously control her inner-psychic mechanisms of regression and progression, felt well held in the relationship with me, and had herself gathered experiences as to which resources had been confirmed or were available to her for stabilization and self-analysis purposes.

Ms. S. prepared a trauma map, and we decided to work through the situation of the first sexual abuse by her alcoholized father by means of the EMDR procedure (see Hofmann, 1999). For Ms. S., this was accompanied by an experience of maximum stress and a very low positive self-attribution (SUD 10, VOC 2 – see Hofmann, ibid.). Her depressive self-degradation was reflected in the sentences of the child that she "herself was to be blamed and was completely worthless". We had a total of seven EMDR sessions dealing with two different abuse situations, until the patient thought that the thickest knots had at that point been unravelled, and that we now could agree again upon verbal and movement analytical therapy sessions.

During the EMDR sessions, two particularities were of importance: During a dramatic intrusion phase, Ms. S. swayed very strongly on her chair, on the verge of toppling over during the EMDR. I stopped the session temporarily, and we looked for an aid to improve the experience of being held in relation to me as a therapist. We opted for the rope, because Ms. S. had already experienced its holding function during an exercise with the holding rocker. We sat ourselves down on the floor within a closed rope, which the patient used to firmly hold on to when she experienced most serious anxieties; I used my right hand to work as an EMDR stimulator, and my left hand to keep the rope a bit tighter, whenever Ms. S. swayed during a traumatic experience. In this way, the EMDR could be completed successfully in this session.

In another EMDR session, Ms. S. was shaken by heavy crying fits and suffered from heart pain by re-experiencing the traumatic images. Again, we looked for an easy and effective aid to overcome these problems, after we had already decided that she could help her inner child by bringing about a relief of agitation with a "butterfly touch of both shoulders" (see Hofmann, 1999). Here again, the little hedgehog served as an extension of the idea. Keeping the little hedgehog on her lap during the ongoing EMDR procedure, the patient did the butterfly touch with the hedgehog, in order to help the hedgehog to work out its severe experience. Only after "the hedgehog had managed to do this during the EMDR session", was Ms. S. again able to do the remaining work out of the trauma within the framework of an inner role distribution between adult and child.

Following these trauma expositions, we had a number of psychotherapeutic evaluation discussions and tried to comprehend the status of clarifications of present adult relationships. After the patient had really actively helped and made her contribution to the process, she wanted to hug me once tightly, and I allowed her to do this. During another session, Ms. S. also wanted me to hug her, and I did so heartily. From now on, the subject of hugging was absolutely uncomplicated and was even repeated several times, until it was superfluous. But since the influence of the parents was not yet really been brought within healthy (adequate in view of the age) boundaries, in later movement therapeutic sessions we thought about how this subliminal sphere of influence might be reduced even more (see graduated approach under 1.4. above).

After some symbolization associations, Ms. S., who in the meantime also participated in a voluntary group therapeutic work (see 1.3.5 above), decided that her mother might be represented by the "big giant tub" and her father by the "big giant bag" (objects, see annex 4.1), in order to work on the remaining paralysing transferences towards her parents and to safeguard against any further traumatizations by others.

During another therapy session the patient selected the giant tub as a representation of her mother and put it into the movement room. After having scolded her mother, she furiously toppled the tub and kept rolling it through the room – one time pushing it from one corner to the other, another time kicking it from one corner to the other. Having done this, the patient laid herself into the tub as a child, and I was allowed to roll her around in the room several times, as a reward for her courage.

What was important in respect to the external behavior of Ms. S. was that she really did get along more confidently with her mother with her progressed adult behavior, for example in connection with the question of the minimal amount of her financial support, etc.

Ms. S. addressed the question of the understandable negative father transference in a group therapeutic session. Without a word, she jumped head-on into the counter-aggression, giving this neurotically disordered reference figure in a symbolic form numerous kicks in the rear-end which she thundered into the black giant bag. She repeated this procedure in a setting with several group participants who demonstrated their mutual solidarity on a sisterly or brotherly basis and vented their anger on the "object of the familial betrayal", each of them in an own way.

Due to these movement therapeutic activities, the patient had made good progresses with regard to the subjects of parental dependency and female identity – and especially in her work on the trauma; as a result of this the psychotherapeutic work on the parental introjects was also a bit facilitated – but further efforts were still required.

Therapeutic Outlook for the Case Example of Franka Schulze:
Ms. S. went through several stages of the structural universal individual and group psychotherapy, which formed a coordinated sequence both logically and disorder-specifically. In the meantime, she has finished both therapy forms with me quite successfully.

The subject of sexual abuse hasn't caused any more psychological strain on Ms. S. since the sessions described above. She was able to maintain her performance in her studies down the line and even improve them, from her point of view, since she didn't any longer study in such a compulsory and ineffective way and was able to see a grade of "B" really as "adequately good". She has had clarifying discussions with her parents in the meantime, which she had mastered without relapsing into old anxiety and flight structures. She refrained from bringing a charge against her father because of the many years of sexual abuse, because she didn't want to pay the tribute of any renewed emotional turmoil any more, and also because her father has also started a psychotherapy.

Therapeutic Summary of the Case Example of Franka Schulze:
The development of Franka S. described above shows important structural phases. At first, the therapeutic aim with regard to this patient with her comprehensive negative parent transferences and the central subject of a traumatic abuse was to establish in a benevolent verbal and activity-oriented way a trustful relationship atmosphere in respect to the patient's infantile (regressive) and adult (progressive) inner-psychic level of regulation. To that end, we used simple contact-oriented and resource-oriented oscillation possibilities in the form of contact sticks, holding rocker, children's swing, hammock, and stuffed animal dialogues.

After about 40 sessions, it became evident in a stuffed animal dialogue (described above) that the patient wanted to establish a physical contact with me. Since this self-active initiative was still afflicted with anxieties, I "broke down" the envisaged activity into a "nested establishment of contact" of the stuffed animals, so that a certain progress could be anticipated here, which might be achieved in the therapeutic transference situation, but which at this point would not yet be maintained in the therapeutic transference situation. For the same reason, I did not yet consent to the desired hugging of Ms. S. at an earlier point, which she had expressed as a fantasy, because a physical contact experience, "which has not yet been established internally", may quickly lead to a longer therapeutic relapse. The girl had then always forgiven her real father too early and trusted him again, because she did not want to do without his affection or was not able to do without it because of her emotionally even more unreliable mother.

Once the well-established ability to differentiate had grown in therapy, and both, the girl Franka and Mrs. Schulze, were able to touch my hand and did not have to deny or to repress it shamefully in the following sessions, I thought the time for trauma exposition had come.

During the EMDR sessions, there are relatively quick coping mechanisms due to the good inner preparation (only seven sessions for the traumatic subject). Twice, therapy objects help to stabilize the patient: At first, the "practical connectedness" between the suffering child and the therapy father can be felt and used in a stabilizing way by means of a rope. Then, a serious psychic scene to be dealt with can be worked on through a by now well-practiced breakdown, where the adult (Mrs. Schulze as an oriented framework person), the assistant therapist (the assistant adult carrying out the EMDR and holding the hedgehog), and the suffering child (here, the EMDR hedgehog and the regressive child) are given the possibility of working successfully on the traumatic low.

When stuffed animals are used during a regressive and symbolic conversation scene, they are transformed to transitional transference objects for parent-child-relationships, because they provide the possibility of dialogues which to some extent reflect the anxieties of the psychically impaired child and at the same time help to compensate earlier deficits on an experimental basis, since the parents never played with the child in such a way.

Besides this filling and nourishing effect, such dialogues also have a testing character for the new growth of the relationship (e.g. "nested hand contact").

The transitional transference objects of the tub and of the black giant limp bag gave the patient the possibility of symbolizing her infantile experience and of working on her aggression subsequently or of anticipating of a pubertal shaping of the patient's relationship to her parents, which would have less respect for their affective power.

Case Example of the Patient Martin Ellert *:
Mr. E. is about 30 years old, a lecturer in foreign languages, and unmarried. He came to me looking for a psychotherapy because of panic-like anxiety states and serious problems referring to his self-esteem.

During the anamnesis of the intellectually very sophisticated patient, it could be worked out that Mr. E. had probably been traumatically damaged secondarily as a result of the very similarly structured panic anxieties of his mother. It seemed to me that deep war traumata resulting from World War I and World War II had possibly been left untreated. As a consequence of this, the mother had in later years just "slipped away without any serious cause" in many trifling situations which occurred in the family, i.e. she dissociated into anxiety states which were shaped by a relative self-dynamic.

Since *nobody explained anything* to the boy and the family just wanted to "keep him out of" all that, the boy soon got into unspecific anxiety states, where he as a little child worried about his mother's life and the life of the addiction endangered and fragile father. His empathetic fantasies intensified to such an extent that one could speak of a secondary traumatization, because Mr. E.'s symptoms included visual panic images (intrusion-like), a frequent hyperarousal of the body, nightmares, and constant feelings of ambivalences toward the indirectly and unspecifically experienced disorder images with his parents.

In my opinion, his symptoms did not fully meet the criteria of a post-traumatic stress disorder – but they were near. That means we were dealing with a secondary (infected) traumatization within the framework of a neurotic relationship conflict with signs of parentification on the part of the patient. The psychodynamic work charts of Mr. E. were as follows:

Table 10:

Transference/Introject on the basis of		Dimension in the Patient's Experience and Behavior	
		Transference	Introject
Mother	the patient's point of view	I am constantly afraid of an accident in the near future or of mistakes, because I can't pre-determine the feelings of others and of my own.	I react passively and dra-matically in the case of simple problems.
	the therapist's point of view	I worry about many people and facts, because I believe I depend on them existentially.	I am passive and tend to seek the attention of others aggres-sively, when I am not so well.
Father	he patient's point of view	I am afraid not to meet the stan-dards or expectations of others, because I fluctuate so much when it comes to my abilities.	I am short-tempered and tend to depreciate others egocen-trically, if I don't understand the other one.
	the therapist's point of view	I have fears of failure, because I tend to ignore my achieve-ments and to subordinate myself quickly to others.	I am short-tempered and sometimes hot-tempered, if I feel ignored by a loved one.
Psychodynamic Work Chart			
Focus	he patient's point of view	I am afraid to make mistakes or not to meet the standards or expectations of others, because I believe that my existence depends on my perfection and the affection of others.	
	the therapist's point of view	I believe myself to be dependent on all people and that I have to serve their moods, because I do not experience any justification for my inner feelings and can't imagine that others really like me when it comes to the establishment of boundaries.	

Ways of Solution / Limits	he patient's point of view	• My job must not be put at risk. • The therapy should not labilize me personally and should not increase my anxieties. • The therapist should join me in doing difficult exercises and should not leave me alone. • The movement exercises should contribute to a physical relaxation
	the therapist's point of view	• The patient is very afraid of any labilizations and could slow down the process as a result of a worsening of the symptoms. • The patient must have positive motherly and fatherly relationship offers or transference offers. • Attention has to be paid to the danger of retraumatization of the inner child when working on the parental disorder images.

In view of the patient's external adjustment and the extremely excessive demands he made on himself versus his inner loneliness and instability, I organized the first therapy sessions very psycho-educationally in terms of "thinking and feeling out loud". In this way, I wanted to ensure that the patient got as much insight as possible into the structure of a therapy session, the reasons for the setting based on the diagnostic knowledge at the moment, and the derivation of the movement sequences. At the end of a therapy session, we usually scheduled about 10 minutes to summarize the session and to "translate" small tasks for everyday life. This procedure already demonstrated that I was different from his parents, because they had often left the boy alone with his emotions.

Besides the discussion of everyday subjects always had "the highest conflict alarm stage" for the patient, we were occupied in therapy almost 40 sessions with easy contact and stabilization techniques, and in this connection his own contributions to the establishment of the setting was of greatest importance to me. Since he often claimed right away that he had no good ideas, I tended to drop an "unspecific half idea" now and then and have it completed by the patient.

So I said, for example, that the giant egg could also be a good way to experience the feeling of being sheltered and safe, and I rolled it towards the patient. So, he was forced to react at least a bit and look into the egg. Then I said something to the effect that it was sometimes good to have a large egg alone just for oneself and not have to share it with someone else, but that it would sometimes be really fun, when many guests (while I pointed at the stuffed animals) came to visit.

Whatever the patient decided to do, I always tried to comment a lot and to support many decisions as a spontaneous and correct selection. I often asked him which position he wanted me to assume when accompanying his self-exploration process, and when he hesitated I would help him by proposing two or three alternatives. The aim was to help Mr. E. to come into contact as much as possible with the reciprocal responses with regard to the objects and to me, and this ultimately helped to reduce or to stop his strong external orientation.

In the giant egg situation the patient decided to use it as a "children's playhouse", and he invited me to visit him together with a penguin. Next, I asked him whether he wanted me to bring along either a fish or a dictionary (alluding to his job), and he replied: "a fish, of course". And the dialogue continued in this way.

The dialogues served as a kind of fun ping-pong, which was designed to divert the fearful patient from his anxiety-laden world of symptoms. Exercises with rods, a swing, a rope, and balls served the purpose of further strengthening the patient and of establishing contact.

Apart from that, the patient liked the hammock exercises so much that he immediately bought one for himself and used to swing at home "across the room of his apartment" in his leisure time. Shortly before the end of the therapy session, Mr. E. often organized the holding rocker for himself for a holding exercise in the relationship. Playing with balls was also impressive for him, because his father either didn't want to play with a ball or had been completely unskilled in this respect.

After these therapy sessions had obviously been effective in terms of a mood improvement and a performance improvement, as well as in terms of establishing a more stable relationship to me, the aim after these about 40 sessions was to work more specifically on the above-mentioned focus in three stages.

In the next session I asked Mr. E. to enact the focus of the relationship disorder with a parent (or with both parents) by means of an object. The patient spoke loudly, as if to himself, that he experienced his mother especially as a burden and that he kept moving in a circle in this respect. Having said this, I asked the client to take an object as a burden on to his shoulders and just to walk around in a circle. Mr. E. took the medium-sized black limp bag (see appendix 4.1) and carried it around in a circle. While doing so, he said that he was unable to really grab the bag, which, of course, also applied to his mother. He continued to walk around in a circle, and I kept silent after having given him a final instruction that he should continue to think of his mother, carry the bag around, and speak loudly. Hardly any changes were to be noted for about 5 minutes. He just kept carrying the bag patiently and strolling around.

Then slowly but surely annoyance emerged. The patient continued to walk around in a circle carrying the bag on his shoulders, but now he began to scold his mother, his family, the war, etc., at first in a low voice, then louder. Since the bag became quite heavy after about 10 minutes of walking, sometimes, stooped, his verbal statements became harsher. Yet, he kept carrying his burden around "like a faithful donkey".

After another two minutes he asked me whether we could have a break. I said that the session was not yet finished and that the problem had not yet been solved. As a consequence, he became even more furious – this time also with me, accusing me of just "standing there so unsympathetically", etc. After another minute, he flew off the handle: Throwing the bag on the floor, he said that "everybody – his mother, his father, and obviously me too, that all of us were crazy, because we put such excessive demands on him – without any consideration!" I gave him the time to have his fill of the affect, then, since the session would be over in a minute, I said, that we would talk about it the next time.

As a consequence, the patient started to establish some important boundaries in the relationship: He cancelled the (requested) visit Christmas in favor of a dancing party with friends, and he took a two-week break in the therapy to finally be able to spend a few restful and relaxing days at the sea.

In the second focus-oriented therapy stage, we concentrated on the traumatizing memory and fantasy images by means of the screening technique (see Huber, 2003 a, b). To that end the patient imagined seeing the fearful and panicked face of his mother and the hot-tempered face of his father on a screen.

If the anxiety was very high, the patient would stamp his feet loudly while seated or he would pound a bag with the club he had available as an acoustic diversion to destroy the pattern of the stimuli. He did the same with the war images in his fantasy which had taken hold of him almost as "self-experienced (fantasy) memories", because his parents had so frequently talked about their war experiences and memories. As if he were dealing with a projectionist, Mr. E. shouted: "Stop the film!". During this exposition of the traumatic material, the client suddenly recalled that his father had once been sitting in the bathroom threatening to commit suicide, while his mother had desperately been praying that he would live on.

These recollections and the "slow motion process" during the screening exposition proved to be an important lever for the patient's development, because he now learned to have *true empathy* with the little boy who had been confronted with excessive demands made upon him, and the patient came to the point where he could understand him better in the disorder as an adult.

In the third focus-oriented therapy stage I suggested to the patient that he would be able to establish even more boundaries with respect to the disorders of his parents, if he represented the structure of their neuroses in the form of objects. He should then enter into an honest dialogue with them, in which he should act as little Martin's attorney. Mr. E. resolved this little "court hearing" brilliantly with good statements off the cuff. As a representation of his mother he selected the giant bag – and for his father the giant block. When assuming the roles of the parents, the patient spoke with caricatured voices – almost like a parody on them.

The attorney sentenced both parents to apologize to the boy and to undergo an in-patient psychotherapy, etc.

Therapeutic Outlook for the Case Example of Martin Ellert:
Following the phase of the contact and resource-oriented therapy sessions, Mr. E. also joined the quarterly group meetings of a closed walk-in group at our practice (see 1.3.5 above), where he also learned to establish other social contacts in contrast to his old neurotic dependency structures. He has a girlfriend now and also learned to appear more firmly as a lecturer in front of his students.

His father and his mother didn't make any therapeutic efforts, but simply dismissed their son as "egoistic" (father) and "heartless" (mother), which has allowed the patient to live more peacefully. Panic symptoms don't hardly matter any more.

Therapeutic Summary of the Case Example of Martin Ellert:
The above therapy process shows a gradual approach to the focuses of the treatment in terms of the therapeutic relationship and the movement structures. Since Mr. E. reveals a lot of anxieties, avoidance behavior, and strong self-depreciative tendencies, I have to first spend a lot of time and make every effort in order to establish a positive contact within the framework of a positive parental transference, so that the patient will really – i.e. practically experienceable – feel accepted by and comfortable with me.

To that end I choose in my contact with the patient the communication style of dealing with a small child, so that I can comment as much as possible and make transparent as much as possible what is going on inside me (reflection of affects, transparency of thoughts). But at the same time, I also inform the patient on an adult level about the general therapeutic reasons and the structure for these therapy steps so that the patient doesn't belittle himself and doesn't artificially feel dependent and passively taken care of.

After evidences that our relationship is therapeutically treatable, I try to lead the patient in the direction of working closer on the treatment focuses.

The independent symbolized activity-specific performances are of vital importance in this connection.

The bag on the client's shoulders then becomes the "beseelte" expression of the neurotic experience of his problem. With the intensification of the burden-anger-feeling, the bag then becomes a transitional transference object in this scene. Throwing off the bag is a creative model solution for the problem resolution he is striving for, which will be brought about as a solution by the patient himself by his mobilizing his own experience resource.

After these successful experiences, the therapeutic progress then leads into the focus of the trauma exposition work with the screening method, which will finally be brought to a close with the performed gestalt therapeutic court hearing. The more independent patient will grow out of the dynamic relationship to the therapist (father) and turn to a pubertal phase in the form of a participation in a group therapy and of changes in his external behavior in his peer groups.

2.1.4 Case Examples of Experimental Focus-Related Work on Inner-Psychic Problems

In the course of an advanced psychotherapy, it will be decreasingly necessary and purposeful to formulate a narrow therapy focus. Often only the framework subject is determined and it gets checked in its variations in everyday life – i.e. "on the accidental coincidence of today's encounter with the therapist" within the therapy session. The patient is accustomed to seeing himself in various transference and introject roles and is also able to allocate the therapist to different perception roles of the setting.

The basis of any experimental focus work is a fundamentally good therapeutic working relationship between the client and the treater. This means, of course, that it may also be impossible on some therapy days to do any experimental performance work because of a current relationship conflict, but one can frequently sense this only at the beginning of a therapy session.

Due to the accumulation of jointly experienced therapy performances and evaluation sessions, transferences, introjects, and focuses will often become more variable. As a consequence of this, there will no longer be such important differences between the perception of the patient and the therapist. Any differences in their respective mutual interpretations will be expressed more openly and sometimes also negotiated cooperatively. Therefore, the individual differences in the opinions will now no longer be emphasized in the psycho-dynamic work charts, but instead more attention can now be paid to the diversity of the impressions that have been collected.

Any progress in basic insights can entail like clockwork structural behavior analyses and, if applicable, changes of behaviour, for which the first preparatory foundations had been laid here.

Second Case Example of the Patient Martin Ellert:
The patient's psycho-dynamic work charts were described above (see 2.1.3.1). I would now like to explain a therapy sequence in which Mr. E. had already worked in an experimental focus-oriented setting. Having devoted quite a number of performances to the focuses of carrying the burdens for others, adopting anxieties from others, and bowing oneself to the fate of the family (see above), ramifications of these subjects or an experimental exploration of some unclear psychic symptoms were now on the agenda as the target of our investigations, before the therapy should be brought to a close.

In a therapy session Mr. E. started to talk of a dream which bothered him, because he had dreamed that he had almost died. In his dream he had been lying under a huge rock and observed from a third party's point of view how he got increasingly weaker and started to anticipate his death, almost with a smile on his lips.

After a short discussion about a possible performance, we represented the scene he had experienced in his dream by means of objects: Next to him was a large rock (the giant block) and another one was laid across his body (the giant limp bag – see appendix 4.1). At first, Mr. E. had difficulties to get in the right frame of mind, so that I repeated in a calm and earnest voice his experience. Now, the state of anxiety began to re-emerge slowly.

Mr. E. had the feeling that he was about 10 years old, and under the burden of the rock he could hardly felt his flat breathing. In a distressed and an infantile way he spoke of his feelings of helplessness. Suddenly, a smile flitted across his face, and I asked him, what he was experiencing right then. The patient replied that he now saw himself again from the perspective of a third party, like a little worm under a rock. I asked him how old the observer now was. He said that he was 12 or 13 years old. Next I asked him whether the big boy didn't feel sorry for the little 10 year old boy who was lying so helplessly under the rock. The bigger boy said no, not really – and anyway, the pressure was not too intense; he would only help in the most extreme cases of emergency.

Changing direction, I now turned to the 10 year old boy and asked him whether he could see the older boy. The little boy in the patient said yes, he could see the boy but that he was an arrogant asshole. I confirmed the impression he had at the moment, adding, however, that the heavy rock might possibly only be removed with their joint strength. The 10 year old boy doubted the solidarity of the older boy and didn't know what to do.

After a while I suggested that I might intensify the pressure on the rock so that we could see what would then happen with him and with the older boy. He should just use his hands and feet and try to fight against it. The little boy agreed and I pressed my fists on the bag from above. The boy groaned and tried to defend himself a bit. I encouraged him to utter a sound more loudly and mobilize more strength to press against it. The little boy indeed mobilized a bit more strength.

Then I laid the whole upper part of my body on the giant bag, pressing it down still more vigorously, while encouraging the little boy further to mobilize still more strength to defend himself against it. The little boy became more furious, stronger, and suddenly he yelled in a relatively male voice. I told him that could open his eyes even more and could be even louder. When the patient intensified his efforts and loudness, I reduced the pressure which I exerted with the upper part of my body on to bag. Finally, the aggressively thawed patient pushed the giant bag away, with furious waves of his arms and legs, which I allowed him to do. We were both sweating quite a lot as a result of the efforts, and we smiled.

Finally, I still asked the patient how many parts there had been now when pushing the bag away? Mr. E. said that in the end he hadn't noticed any more any split, but that he had defended against the pressure with "full strength", otherwise he wouldn't have been able to win.

Therapeutic Outlook for the Second Case Example of Martin Ellert:
Mr. E. was very impressed after this session how he had suddenly come to understand his psychic defense. He had vividly experienced, as he explained in our subsequent follow-up discussion, that he "consisted of several levels" and that both the helpless little boy and the contemptuous older boy belonged to him.

As an interpretation, a breakdown in terms of helplessness and of a complicated interaction between the transference child Martin and the father-introject (consisting of Martin and the father) came to his mind. The father had just watched idly (like the red giant block) how the boy had been "besieged" by his mother (the giant bag). These interpretations were worked out in more detail during the following four therapy sessions and supported with the evidence of case examples.

As a consequence, the patient was again able to see the disorder of his parents and his own hopeless position as an unprotected child in this neurotic family constellation.

The enormous strength he had mobilized had given the patient an impetus which had been triggered by his experience that he had simply pushed away "even the therapist together with the black bag" by mobilizing all his resistance.

He was able to live from this powerful example for a long time.

Therapeutic Summary to the Second Case Example of Martin Ellert:
In this experimental focus-oriented therapy session, Mr. E. was able to purposefully re-perform his symbolic dream experience at a decisive point in the therapy.

As the therapist I could have just organized a verbal evaluation work when the therapy objects, the giant bag and the giant block, were selected. But since the point is mostly the whole "character of the activity-specific performance", I consciously decided to let the patient control the process, at least up to the point where I believed an important "dead center" of the acting character was apparent. When the boy psychically "broke down into the helpless, motionless boy and the observing degrader", I thought it was necessary to intervene therapeutically in order to avoid any subsequent re-traumatizing experiences (as fearfully pointed out in the dream).

When the patient associated the older boy with the age of 12 or 13, I thought that this was the time when this dissociation had brought about a psychic relief for the real boy who felt strained by the excessive demands which had been made on him. On the other hand, I already assumed at this point – due to the previous focus-oriented work – that a father introject would also push its way into the re-performance and demonstrate vividly what had happened in the family-dynamically sense back then.

Be that as it may, in this current performance it was necessary to let the little boy experience an increase in strength. Out of mindfulness of the inner dynamics on the part of the boy, I didn't want to do this quasi externally, because such supporting actions mostly only lead to short-term developmental successes. Interesting to me was the older boy's statement that he "would only help in the most extreme cases of emergency". Therefore, I opted for the strategy of putting the inferior boy a bit more under pressure (without tormenting him sadistically!), so that the bigger one would finally intervene.

When I requested the little boy to mobilize all his strength and use his hands and feet to defend himself, this was surely also a moment giving him a positive fatherly strength. Due to this suggestive challenge, I demanded full concentration for the performance from the boy; in this way, dissociations can sometimes be "made undone". The plan was successful, and the increasingly stronger boy mobilized all his strength to defend himself against the pressure. Since this experiment had worked well, I still intensified the resistance with the upper part of my body a bit so as to give the patient an even greater sense of achievement, because it enabled him to sense his enormous subliminal strength (of which he had so far been unaware).

These subsequent verbal considerations prove in my opinion that this re-performance entailed a good activity-specific analysis and opened the possibility of a desired synthesis of change in the patient's behavior.

2.1.4.1 Case Examples of Experimental Focus-Related Work on Traumatic Pathology

In order to be able to implement an experimental focus-oriented therapy setting with traumatized patients, it is, of course, necessary, as described above in 2.1.4, to verify a safe relationship-dynamic work between the patient and the therapist so that this emotionally difficult to predict experience material can be adequately treated in a professional way. That means that the client should also be verbally informed on the emotional level about the trauma to be worked on, and should have proven in previous sessions that he or she is able to deal relatively safely with any spontaneously emerging experience material. And finally, it should also be possible for the patient to participate in controlling the relationship to the therapist in terms of a positive orientation, i.e. with a good interest of clarification and his or her own auxiliary therapeutic contributions.

Such a therapeutic working level was present from my point of view in following case examples.

Case Example of the Patient Renate Brandt *:
Mrs. B. is about 40 years old, a self-employed health professional, and married. Mrs. B. came to me looking for a therapy because of depressive symptoms, aggression inhibitions, and continuous psychosomatic complaints (headaches and heart pains). Years ago, she had already done an analytical psychotherapy in a classical setting by which she had been able to achieve an increase in independency and a reduction of suicidal impulses. As she told me, the negative transference relationships to her (female) therapist had unfortunately been difficult to resolve, and also, their work on the causes of the disorders had only taken place in "the mind". Therefore, she now wanted to have a second go at doing a therapy, and this time with a movement-oriented therapy.

After the patient had already worked on basic problems referring to her father and her mother as well as on the basic psychosomatic connections relating to her problems in focus-oriented therapy sessions, she wanted to address the traumatic experience of physical violence, for which memories were, however, so far missing.

In a therapy session, the patient decided that she wanted to try once to trace certain physical symptoms on the basis of a stuffed animal dialogue. She had already experienced such a stuffed animal dialogue before with me as a creative and casual form of communication. In this connection, it had been a pleasant experience for her to see that one could talk about most difficult subjects more openly in a third party's role by means of stuffed animals than it would have been possible on the basis of an adult verbal dialogue. When trying to explore on an adult level, the well-known transference patters quickly turned up again, and they could only be reduced slowly in spite of the interpretations and insights that had been worked out. The idea was that, by shifting the relationship setting it might be possible to gain *an experimental insight into the backgrounds of the disorders* (in the sense of a preview), where it probably would have taken much longer to work out our real relationships in the current transference and introjection.

Our contact and resource-oriented therapy encounters had demonstrated to me in a convincing way that the patient was able to establish a sustainable relationship to me in transference-scarce encounter spaces; in addition, she had proven her self-analytical therapy competence to me during our focus-oriented work.

Today, Mrs. B. selected a little lion for herself and a fatherly big brown bear for me. Following this allocation, I asked in the role of the bear how the little lion was today. The little lion answered that it wasn't bad today, but that it still had such heavy neck pain – for years now. The bear asked where exactly the pain was located in the head and how bad it was. Mrs. B. pinched the little lion very violently on its neck and pressed the animal's face flatly down on the floor, and then she threw the little lion vigorously into the corner of the room.

At first, I was a bit surprised and asked her, whether she had understood my last question. Mrs. B. answered in a somewhat infantile (regressed) voice, yes, but that it had been so! I asked her again what exactly had happened and went to the corner to get the little lion. I handed it over to Mrs. B. and asked her to repeat again in slow motion what had happened before and accompany her action by commenting aloud what she thought and felt at that moment, so that I could get a better understanding of it.

She agreed, took the little lion and explained that she was now pressing the neck of the stuffed animal lion as firmly as she felt the pain at that moment. I asked her, whether she could close her eyes for a moment, sense who it was who seized the little lion so brutally in the neck. The patient cried and said that she could feel the old woman or her father behind her. (The old woman had once been the nanny of the family, who, as I found out later, had presumably been a neuropathic person resettled from Eastern Europe, and who had often looked after the children of the very busy parents alone.)

Then I asked the patient whether she had an idea what had caused this violence. The lion replied (with a gesture) and in the infantile voice of the patient, that she had just vomited and that her face was now being dipped into the vomit. Parallel to this, the patient pressed the stuffed animal's face again flatly on the floor, and then she threw it violently into the corner. Having fetched the little lion cautiously again, I asked the patient whether we could still work a bit in "slow motion". The patient nodded in dismay. I asked her if she knew even more about the old woman or the father in that scene.

The patient said, that at the age of two or four she often been scolded by the old woman because she vomited food, because, as the old woman said, "other children would be happy and thankful, if they had had anything at all to eat". (As an expellee the old woman had probably experienced a lot of famine and violence herself.) But at that point the story becomes blurred, because the patient can't remember whether it was this woman or her father or someone else who had pressed her face into the vomit and thrown her into the corner. She had been under an apathetic shock at that time and lost her bearings.

She said she remained lying down like dead in her vomit and blood from a nosebleed, in the scene she had just remembered. She didn't know any more how long she had been lying there – an eternity; there wouldn't be any resolution of the scene and no more certainty about the details of what really happened, because she had been under a shock.

In any case, she had always been very afraid of her father's and her nanny's outbursts of fury. She had been terrified of that nanny, but hadn't told her parents anything of this. She added that her parents would flip out quickly, if something had not been in accordance with their wishes.

At the end of the therapy session, I asked the patient to build a little sick-bed for the little lion and to say goodbye to the little lion till next time.

In the next therapy session, Mrs. B. suddenly recalled her early leave-taking of her dead brother. Her brother's odor, appearance, and the melody of his manner of speaking emerged as a real memory at that moment. Now, she also built a little bed for him out of clay in the form of a little sculpture. And then she took the time to go to the far-off cemetery in order to consciously say goodbye to him for the first time in a moving ritual.

Hypothetically, she guessed that possibly her own experience and her brother's experience – at a time when she was two years old – had been combined in the image of violence that had been directed towards the sick child.

Her brother had died in great pain as a result of faulty surgery because of a burst appendix.

Therapeutic Outlook for the Case Example of Renate Brandt:
After this therapy performance, Mrs. B. was upset for days and built a little bed for a bent little child out of clay (see above: working with therapy figures under 1.3.4). By doing so, she consciously assumed the responsibility of looking after both physically abused children.

If I hadn't persistently inquired, then there would possibly only have been the action – without any comment, since the emotional recollection only got going after I had retrieved the little lion. The impulses had been unclear up to that point, just as the headache and neckache had been unspecific. After the activity-specific performance, the patient had even more headaches at first, and she had to cry a lot. Now, she hadn't had any pain for several days. It was, however, clear to her hypothetically that her headache and neckache could have something to do with inconsiderate relationship experiences.

In the current session, as pain sensations increased, Mrs. B. reacted to small incidents by quickly having the feeling of being badly treated which previously had really been different. In the meantime, she has in general become resentful towards her parents who hadn't cared about the psychic stability of her nanny and had just been "happy about the reduction of the workload" with regard to the child care, or also because of her parents' arguments with the flipping out of the father. With regard to her pain referring to her brother, the ritualized subsequent funeral had helped her, because as a child she had not been allowed to participate in her brother's funeral and thus say goodbye in a dignified way. Possibly she had also adopted a part of his agonies, as she said afterwards.

Anyway, it was astonishing that Mrs. B.'s anxieties with respect to not being able to fall asleep and not being able to sleep uninterruptedly all night had completely disappeared *after these therapeutic and real performance structures.* To that end, she didn't need drugs or the presence of family members any more, and she experienced an increase in strength and power as an adult, liberated woman.

Therapeutic Summary of the Case Example Renate Brandt:
The activity-specific performance demonstrates impressively how fertile a verbalization of movement impulses by means of symbolizing objects can be. Mrs. B. had revealed rough correlations between deprivations on the part of the parents and violence in her upbringing. Any further, exclusively verbal work would in this case only have confirmed the recognitions already

known – possibly in the sense of "clichés".

So far it had not been possible to reveal any further correlations with the physical symptoms or the "reading of the physical experience messages".

The stuffed animal dialogue enabled the patient to approach a difficult traumatic experience relatively relaxed at first with a sort of "dismayed aloofness" and to approach the stressful scene playfully, quasi accidentally.

Following a first impulse, Mr. B. had unconsciously shown a behavior which she had experienced herself but which she couldn't remember. She enacted the bad experience almost incidentally, without having a conscious foreboding of it at that moment. Only after repeating the scene in slow motion several times, did the patient's memory also responded emotionally to it. As the therapist, I didn't know anything more than the patient at that moment. I had just stumbled over the quick sequence of spontaneous actions, which I was unable to explain against the background of my careful observations, and which I considered to be unconsciously controlled in view of the quick sequence.

During the slow re-performance, the structure of violence the child had experience became increasingly more visible. Then the story re-appeared like an "aha-experience" and only had to be caught.

The retrieving of the little lion was, in its relevance for the therapeutic relationship, on the one hand a thoughtful countertransference on my part for the maltreated child and thus a certain (unconscious) contrast experience to the frequent ignorance on the part of her parents. On the other hand, this double throwing away by the child was probably also an indirect relationship test in order to verify whether I would really take care of her so persistently. Possibly, this conflict of throwing away might also have been the indirect relationship battle with the perpetrator introject of the old woman or of her father, where the point would then have been to see who would ultimately succeed with which action. The patient also agreed with this third interpretation, because she realized in her everyday behavior how she often had treated herself badly without being aware of a real reason to do so. The model-like adopted introjects of the father and the old nanny might be an unconscious explanation in this respect.

Furthermore, a part of her brother's agonizing death and of the unmastered leave-taking of him was also encoded in this nested performance. The memory was only triggered after the "cover story" had been revealed, which explained why the "little sister had been unable to come to rest for years". In the real performance, a humanely very important leave-taking action was enacted, which Mrs. B. had been denied before by her unempathetic parents.

In the therapeutic performance, the little lion and the big brown bear became transitional transference objects for a careful parent-child-interaction, where important psychosomatic correlations were explored on the basis of a sensitive activity analysis, which could not be worked out on the verbal level of the adult woman up to that point. A resolution of the repressed pain then finally brought the "psychosomatic rest" she longed for.

2.1.5 Long-Term Case Development in a Structural Universal Individual Psychotherapy

In this case description, the therapy stages of a patient will be outlined, covering a total period of three years. The patient paid most of the therapy himself and successfully worked very independently on the structures of his depressive neurosis. Certain therapy settings which are of key relevance will be emphasized for the purpose of an easy survey. The therapy sculptures shown in the appendix are to illustrate vividly the patient's path of suffering, recognitions, and joys (see appendix under case example 4.2 D. H.).

*Long-Term Case Example of the Patient Detlef Heinel *:*
Mr. H. is about 40 years old, an academic, and married. He came to me looking for a psychotherapeutic treatment because of depressive symptoms with psychosomatic complaints and hypochondriac anxieties. He had previously done an analytical individual psychotherapy in another federal state of Germany, but with little success. His mother had died of cancer a few years earlier, while his father and his brother lived in faraway cities. At first, Mr. H. was a very adapted client with a quick intellectual perceptiveness, which might have been the origin of a part of his defense and his resistance in his previous therapy.

For a better illustration of the patient's disorder structure, the psychodynamic work charts of Mr. H. are shown below, as they had developed and been modified after about one year:

Table 11: Therapy Stage: Contact-Oriented Performances of the Patient Detlef Heinel

Transference/Intro-ject on the basis of	Frame dimension in the Patient's Experience	
	Transference frame	Introject frame
Mother (worked on)	• I must serve everybody, because otherwise nobody will like me. • I am an irreplaceable support for women. • I can't rely on any deep emotions, because moods can destroy everything.	• I believe in rules and laws, although they kill me. • I extort affection from others for me by symptoms of suffering. • I am easy to hurt and tend to degrade in a sneaky way those who frustrate me.
Father (worked on)	• I am unimportant, because the effect I have is too weak. • I can't fulfil other people's expectations. • I must not establish any boundaries, because otherwise I will be rejected	• (Secretly) I think that others are a failure. • (Secretly) I have fantasies of grandiosity. • I flee into physical symptoms so that I don't have to confront anything.
Psychodynamic Work Chart		
Focus (negotiated)	• I must fulfil other people's expectations and serve everybody, because otherwise I am not lovable. • I must not show any aggressions, because otherwise I will be rejected. • Without achievements and rescue operations, I am not seen as a human being.	
Solutions (negotiated)	• Tracking resources of power and strength in the boy and man. • Supporting any expressions of aggression and anger. • Practicing to perceive disappointments, wishes, and needs. • Training to clarify relationships. • Reducing the power of a strong super-ego structure. • Enhancing any creative individual development possibilities.	

Corresponding performances aiming at establishing a contact in the therapeutic relationship were made repeatedly during the first 30 therapy sessions as well as later for orientation purposes in any unclear problem-laden situations of the focus-oriented work or also for relaxation purposes after any strenuous events in later therapy phases. The patient preferred selected contact sticks, the thick rope, the gymnastics ball, the giant tub, and stuffed animal dialogues to that end.

By means of the contact sticks, Mr. H. was able to find out on the basis of three different instructions that he preferred more to adapt himself than to take the lead. In addition, he began to feel at the beginning a "dangerous anger" in his arm movements "which would disturb the harmony", which we in turn redirected in line with the above-mentioned focuses to a contact- and resource-oriented aggression exercise with the red block in the 25th therapy session, and which we could thus use as an activity-specific performance. Noteworthy in this 25th session was that at the beginning Mr. H. could only hit on the red block as a father symbol with my support. But after a few minutes he asked me to also give him the second (my) bataca (foam rubber bat), as he was then already able to attack the block alone or confident that he would manage this open expression of aggression without any support – after such brief joint training.

In another resource-oriented exercise we closed the thick rope by means of a snap hook so that it formed a ring, and we used it for a confidence exercise like a holding rocker (see above case example of Sven Reimann in 2.1.2). Here, it turned out that Mr. H. entered the confidence exercise with the readiness to take a risk, and at the same time was always concerned about the therapist's well-being so that he could hardly enjoy the exercise for himself the first few times.

We used the gymnastics ball in order to do some performances. Here, the patient experienced the therapist's following his exercise proposals as a very joyful, infantile present; the fingerball was connected with an even greater emotion.

Whenever the patient turned out to be in a psychic need later, we were able to achieve an emotional contact in our relationship and an improvement of his stability quickly again simply by means of mere finger contact exercises. The giant tub was also a preferred location in the contact setting for practicing the patient's favorite finger contacts. In the case of the tub, Mr. H. could really stand upright (i.e. be an adult) according to his wishes and consciously establish contact with me.

In later therapy phases, stuffed animal dialogues were usually the most uncomplicated and at the same time emotionally most resonating way to re-establish contact between us or to look for any new accesses to a therapy focus which had matured enough emotionally to be currently worked on. Usually, Mr. H. chose the little curious or sad tiger as an identification figure, either for a talk to his young self or for an orientating dialogue with me (the brown bear). The result of this talk was then the basis for a new initiative.

Therapy Stage: Resource-Oriented Performances of the Patient Detlef Heinel:
In the setting of therapeutic work, resource-oriented performance settings

often follow contact exercises. In the case of Mr. H. my aim up to about the 50th session and prior to the strenuous focus-oriented work was to find out where his stabilizing powers were hidden, what his creative resources as a child and/or an adult looked like, and which interaction structure would be repeated in the relationship to the therapist.

That means that behavior sequences which have been connected are not further developed here for a possible formulation of the treatment focuses, but instead the aim is to determine any short-term tension-reducing intervention structures.

In the case of Mr. H. the following were therapeutically helpful methods for building up psychic power: Batacas and club for hitting, the holding rocker, swinging on the swing and in the hammock, hanging over the giant tub's "belly", and ritualized stuffed animal dialogues between the little tiger and the big brown bear, which had already proven useful in connection with the contact exercises. The only difference was that nothing new was explored here but only used as a stress-reducing resource on the basis of repetitions.

As a general orientation, it was clear to Mr. H. and to me that any resource-enhancing work also has an anti-depressive effect, because it enhances positive self-experiences and helps to establish a positive transference relationship between the patient and the therapist, which they later have to live off when it comes to difficult performance work, where the relationship ability is stressed through negative misappreciations or actions in various settings.

Besides, the patient's psychic ability to differentiate will also be trained discreetly in this stress-free setting. When aggressive impulses emerged in the contact setting with the wooden sticks described above, I didn't start working on the causes (focus) already at this point in view of the structure of the resources, but instead for a short-term acting out of the movement impulses, while at the same time offering my activity-related support. The fact that the patient accepted this supporting offer very joyfully showed me that I was absolutely on target (in addition to the previous agreement) with regard to the orientation of resources in this therapy stage.

When changing the setting during the above contact performance, Mr. H. wanted me to hit the red block with a bataca together with him, and so I did in time with him in order to enhance his rhythm. After a break and after he had thought a short time about it, the patient said that he wanted to hit alone, taking from me the second bataca. The hits became more vigorous and were accompanied by powerful loud sounds, what he had not been able to do before.

Hitting with the batacas or, better still, with the large club, was from now on an important resource training for the patient, when he was looking for cognitive clarity for the role-specific statements or other confrontative performances. Usually, it took but two minutes for such a mental tuning in difficult scenes, and then the healthier part of the patient could assume the task of designing the activity-specific performance in question.

Contrary to that, the holding rocker was a constant resource of recovery, of coming to rest again on a balanced level for the patient after sometimes heart-stirringly sad performances. Additionally, it made him understand on the level of a very direct experience in our relationship that I was available to him in a supporting way with my strength and my balance.

Swinging on the children's swing or in the hammock, in principle, served the same purpose for the patient. The only difference was, that this enabled him to gather even more momentum from this exercise than it was possible in an exercise during which he was just standing still. I showed him my connection with him by giving the swing a push with my hands, as he had previously requested, or by keeping the hammock swinging by means of a little rope which I pulled with my hand. What was important was that I as the therapist had supported him with exactly as much strength as the little or bigger child in the patient liked.

In the course of the therapy, the stuffed animal dialogues gained a special multi-functional importance for the patient. First, they served the purpose of establishing contact with the inner child on a regressive basis, as described above, who could then communicate very quickly with the help of the little tiger what the adult Mr. Heinel had previously only been able communicate vaguely and stiffly on a rationalized basis.

Second, the serial dialogues between the little tiger and the big bear proved to be an excellent means of raising the spirits and giving way to a liberating relationship atmosphere between the patient and the therapist. For some time I had the impression: Even if it turns out that there is nothing working any more as a resource, at least we have the relationship between the tiger and the bear, which is unshakably positive. As for the meaning which Mr. H. usually attributed to the dialogue setting, to him is was like a loving relationship between a big and a little brother.

Third, the relaxed and empathetic dialogues between the tiger and the bear often gave important clues for our focus-oriented work, because here the patient was sometimes able to associate more openly than in a verbal setting.

Therapy Stage: Focus-Oriented Performances of the Patient Detlef Heinel:
During this therapeutic part of the work between the 50th and 100th session,

the patient used to enact with my help very precise problem structures by means of the therapy objects, in accordance with the written or verbal focuses which had been worked out and are shown in the above psycho-dynamic work charts or in accordance with the derivations from everyday conversations, in order to transport them into a hypothetically envisaged solution space.

Depending on spontaneously emerging activity impulses, this procedure kept getting mixed in specific situations with experimental focus-oriented work or resource-oriented phases, if the patient was very exhausted after working on a focus. The following focus-oriented activity-specific performances, which have been selected out of a number of successful work units of the patient were important to Mr. H.: Enacting scenes relating to his family of origin and entering into a dialogue with his family of origin by means of therapy objects; dealing with and confronting with his family members in movement therapeutic sequences and role play statements; working on his near-death experience in early childhood by means of the birth egg; and much more of the same.

The procedure in these sessions was that Mr. H. first proposed the subject to be worked on, specified the problem to be focused, and suggested a possible performance, while presenting at the same time his preliminary reasons to that end.

Then I opened the discussion by confirming the current relevance of the subject, the conciseness of the problem, and the design of the setting, or by modifying and sometimes also by questioning all of this, if I believe to recognize from a therapeutic point of view any adverse aspect in the patient's proposal.

When the patient suggested representing the family constellation, I immediately thought it a good idea, because such an illustration made sense to me diagnostically, and in addition I also thought that the dialogue atmosphere which would be represented in extracts might have a reciprocal effect.

Mr. H. looked around in the room for a short time, then he chose the giant red block as a mother symbol. He said that this object was just right to represent his real mother (he experienced in his childhood), because she had been the largest and most important figure in his childhood, where nobody had been able to get around this figure, just the same as with this bulky thing. Besides, red was the signal color of fear for him. Thereafter, the patient went to the black giant limp bag and said it was a very expressive symbol for his father. From the patient's point of view he had proven his limpness by leaving the family together with the patient's brother when the patient was seven years old, and the only thing he cared for afterwards as a visitor had been some super smart and demanding phrases for the patient.

Furthermore, the patient had only been helpless and sad when being confronted with his father, thus the intangibility of the bag and its black color would be absolutely right. For his little brother, Mr. H. chose the yellow bag, because he had been the "golden boy" of his father, and because there had always been arguments with him, what was also symbolized by the punching bag. The patient represented himself as a little colored pillow with the comment that everyone could do with this plaything whatever he or she liked. The patient placed himself as a "little pillow wheel" on an intersection point in the middle between the figures which he had arranged in a semi-circle. From his point of view, this representation was to express that he had always cared about the emotional concerns of others and had received functional orders from everybody. His mother had chosen him as a little messenger of her "sorrowful life", and sometimes she wanted him to be a lovely cuddlesome child, and at other times a really "better man – contrary to his father". His father in turn expected his son to adopt his contemptuous attitude towards women and an unconditional support of his little brother at school, which later even included having to write his brother's diploma thesis.

The brother thought the patient was a mollycoddled coward and an ass, who could be burdened with loads and could be exploited at their father's discretion. All these associations were of a great vivid value to me as a therapeutic observer and much more expressive than the curriculum vitae I had read previously of the then still-rationalizing patient. In an impressive and to me also moving verbalization section, the patient created a model story of how and in which voice, and how persistently, and with which relationship terror the family had internally communicated among each other.

Based on these specific dialogues, I was later able to work out with the patient some clues which indicated that his mother probably was afflicted with a non-treated borderline disorder, and that his father had presumably been an extremely narcissistic psychopath. These symptomatic evidences could in fact only become obvious to me in the patient's real re-performance, since his previous descriptions weren't but an "everyday speech-specific trivialization of the disorder" of his parents. In the following weeks and months, these therapeutic insights were again and again the basis of further focus-oriented work units concerning body movement-specific and verbal conflicts and confrontations with the members of this disordered family of origin.

With the aim of encouraging the patient or of overcoming taboos, the body therapeutic confrontations usually came first, prior to any verbal confrontations. Similar to the case example of Undine Beier (see above 2.1.1.1 and 2.1.2.1), it was important for the patient at first to deprive the objects of their power by simple contact activities and to attack them at first from a safe distance with aggressive actions. Later, the negative power of the transitional transference object was usually brought down by "working on" it with the club or with kicks, so that any helpless infantile regressions were avoided. With the help of resource-oriented actions on the object, Mr. H. was for the first time able to find access to his latent murderous rage as a focus, which had not been accessible to him so far.

Since he could go to the limit of his physical affect in connection with the object, he was soon able to find the adult measure for regulating his emotions and also gained a rational general view for his statements. I suppose the statements would have been much more depressive, if he had made them before the psycho-physical growth in strength. Now, Mr. H. was able to reflect to his object parents in relatively clear words the catastrophic effects of their disordered behavior. He accused both them in some situations which he listed of having abused him psychically and of having suppressed him heavily.

He reproached his brother especially for his egocentric selfishness and his lack of brotherly solidarity. In this connection, it was important for the patient that he could again and again either supplement or repeat these statements in short sequences, because the feeling of liberation as well as my testifying and confirmation was very important to him.

One of the most difficult focus-oriented work units in the course of the therapy was the symbolic re-performance and working on his early near-death experience. He knew from the report of the midwife that when he was born he had been externally dead for a few minutes due to a lack of oxygen and that he had only been brought back to life due to the courageous hot/cold baths the obstetrician had given him. Through dreams, sessions with catathyme image experiences (see Hennig, 1999), and explorations, we had already worked out that the newborn's fears of death were to be associated with the patient's fears of cardiac arrest. The aim of this trial performance was, however, to look for an experience-near way to work on the problem in order to achieve an even more comprehensive resolution of these (in the meantime neurotically hypochondriacally exaggerated) fears. So far, we had not really succeeded in achieving this satisfactorily. Since I was convinced of the patient's psychic capacities to work out problems, which had grown in the meantime, I agreed with the traumatic exposition work in the birth egg.

The client selected the giant egg as an uterus symbol for the performance, a small rope as umbilical cord, and a stuffed animal penguin as an additional mother symbol.

Then he climbed with the penguin into the uterus egg, letting the umbilical cord hang out of the egg, which he asked me to hold symbolically as an emergency rope. Crouching in the egg like an embryo, he began to cry softly after a short time of mental attunement. In his imagination, he saw his mother's face which appeared to be quite apathetic, and the faces of exhausted helpers.

In a later progressed state, he didn't know exactly whether these faces had really existed, or whether his experience had only corresponded with a model scene (see Lichtenberg, 1991).

In the work scene, it appeared to me to be absolutely authentic and very moving in the experience.

The patient began to cry increasingly more vehemently and loudly. Suddenly, the patient's emotion changed to also include anger, and first he threw the penguin and then also the other end of the rope out of the birth egg. Exhausted and urged to do so by an inner drive, he then crawled out of the egg and laid himself on the green giant mat. I offered the heart-breakingly crying patient a hand to hold close to his chest, which he clasped firmly. He was shaken by a heavy crying fit and shouted: "They had already given me up!" or something like that. Then he came to rest slowly and looked at me gratefully.

During a short subsequent conversation and based on the later effect of this focus-oriented activity-specific performance, Mr. H. said that by throwing away the penguin and the umbilical cord he had reproached his mother for her partial responsibility in connection with the trauma of birth for the first time. Before he had not been allowed to blame her, but to the contrary had been forced to show his great gratitude for his survival.

By crawling out of the egg and with the help of my supporting hand on his chest, his second birth had taken place, so to speak, and he was very happy about this. Furthermore, the patient confirmed later that in this helpless situation he had experienced these human faces as in slow motion, which happens quite frequently when re-experiencing a traumatic situation. He had experienced the possibility of stretching out on the green giant mat as an absolute release for him after the "squeezed narrowness of the uterus". From now on this mat was for some sessions "the embodiment of his growing EGO" and thus a "feeling good mat" or a "playground for the tiger and the bear" in later performances.

Therapy Stage: Experimental Focus-Oriented Performances of the Patient Detlef Heinel:
Within the framework of experimental therapeutic activity-specific performances, the majority of which took place as of the 100th therapy session, the patient's general independent self-therapeutic capability to work and the

efficiency of the therapeutic relationship could be clarified by and large and tested. That means that such an intuitive procedure with a broad transference-specific, introject-specific, focus-specific, and solution-specific framework will only be possible in an advanced therapy process. Individual experimental performance units will, however, also take place quite early in situations which are currently free of any transference because of diagnostic research hypotheses and because the patient should be introduced as early as possible to an independent activity-specific analytic work.

In the interests of space in this book, I would like to restrict myself to describing only three selected experimental focus-oriented activity-specific performances which took place in the course of the patient's therapy.

Since the patient was very motivated to do a therapy, experienced in self-analyses, and able to learn, as described above, the first experimental shaping of settings took place as early as after the 30th therapy session with the aim of hypothetically bringing light into the interaction of body and mind.

One day Mr. H. came to me with heavy back extensor symptoms. After a short questioning and clarification of other causes, I asked to represent the symptoms in an activity-specific performance with me. The patient took the medium-sized limp bag and laid himself backwards on it. Parallel thereto he asked me to increase the pressure on his chest by means of the yellow bag. This setting continued for about two minutes, but without any success. Then I interrupted the performance, which I had supported at first in favour of the patient's independence, and said that we should try to find another form of representation.

In addition, I knew from my bioenergetic training that such a kind of back arch could also be an emotional blockade. So I suggested that we simply try the opposite constellation. I asked him to huddle up forward and I would then press the bag onto his back. As we did this, the patient immediately started to cry loudly and movingly. When he was squeezed together, he had suddenly seen an evil face of his mother.

In our supplement discussion, some interesting hypotheses were raised. First, we were able to support the correlation that the mother, in the form of the black bag, had actually been a heavy psychic stress for the patient due the excessive demands she had made upon the child and due to her unpredictable emotionality. According to the hypothesis of that time, the yellow bag could have been the little brother who had troubled the patient with additional pain. In so far, the first performance was also an image for the state of being at someone's mercy; in the second performance, the dynamic image of the conflict he experienced then got flowing. Only after having cried and seen the image of his mother, was the patient able to consciously allocate the activity-specific performance. In the progression of the adult, it was then possible to make systemic allocations, which the little boy hadn't been able to do earlier.

In later experimental performances, the patient wanted to work with the giant tub as a mother symbol. The performance suggestions he made in this connection were oriented on focus and solution. At first he asked me to roll the tub over him several times while he was lying on the floor. I did so, since the above-mentioned setting conditions were given, although I also felt in the countertransference that it was like a paradoxical sadistic test. After I had rolled the tub twice or three times over him, the patient asked me to let the giant tub just lay on his belly. Lying under the burden, he breathed himself into the feeling and soon started to cry, because he again found himself feeling like a little boy. In this state, the patient remembered scenes where he wanted to play with his mother and who then, after initially having complied with his wishes, increasingly "rolled over" him, while turning the actual infantile game into a "let's please Mother game". And for the patient this was an impressive model scene of the mother-child-disorder.

In another performance, the same giant tub served as an experience carrier for new behavioral experiments. In this connection, Mr. H. hanged himself, for example, at the upright standing tub, or he laid himself on the tub like a red-faced spider monkey.

By doing this, he caught up on an infantile devotion or attachment, which had rarely if at all existed for him in his reality. In the third performance, the giant tub was also the preferred location for practicing finger plays, where the patient used the belly area of the tub or the edge of the upright standing tub as a meeting place for our hands. Over and over again, it was obvious that he was both curiously researching and very happy in a childlike way when an encounter had led to a satisfactory contact. His subsequent self-assessment each time was to say that he was now ready to take on experiments, which he had kept back as a child in connection with his real mother, but which he could now subsequently make up for via the medium of the tub.

In another experimental focus-oriented activity-specific performance, Mr. H. used the blue swinging bag (see appendix 4.1). In a therapy phase, At first, in a certain therapy phase he had the feeling that this object was a suitable father symbol to whom he "paid back" in the form of aggression the humiliations he had suffered, sometimes with the club, at other times with the batacas or with his bare fist. When doing this, he recalled one specific dialogue scene after the other, and parallel thereto he became increasingly an attorney of the little Detlef. In these "hearings", he punished the negative father immediately with slaps in the face, etc., if he had again given any cynical or stupid answers in his role (which the patient had allocated to him and which he played himself).

Step by step the patient had worked through the field of unprocessed recollections and justifications of the child, including the pain he had suffered. Now, there was more space for any suppressed longings on the patient's part. Thus he suggested at the beginning of one session that he would now like to hang himself on to my body as a compensation, but I refused to do this, due to my countertransference (too much intertwinedness with the patient). Instead I proposed that he might hug vigorously the blue swinging bag and hang on to it with his whole body; adding, that once the exercise had progressed, I would then be able to touch his clinging hands with my hands without the feeling that any excessive demands were being made on me. The patient accepted my proposal, and soon he was hanging on the blue swinging bag in an infantile regression as if he were hanging on a real father. Then I got closer to him, while verbalizing things, and put my open hands over his clinging "infantile hands". His cold infantile hands quickly became extremely hot. His eyes were shaped by the longing misery of a ten to twelve year old boy.

After two or three minutes, where he had been deeply shaken, the patient recovered again. After the regression Mr. H. said that beyond the initial disappointment that he had not been allowed to hang himself on me directly, it had also been good to be able to follow the entire activity-specific and association process with an alert power of observation. In connection with his wife, he had sometimes also realized that both of them got lost in phases of too much fusion and then no longer knew how long and what and why they had experienced something. Now, he had really become aware of the fact that first a negative transference to the father and then to me as a therapist had been his inner problem. But due to the limited encounter when I touched his hand, this had then again been turned into a positive acceptance. (I present this section here in such a detailed way as a therapist, because these are exactly the moments of differentiation which are so important in the activity-specific performances, and which have a gradual structure-forming effect).

Therapeutic Outlook for the Long-Term Case Example of the Patient Detlef Heinel:
The structural changes to be noted in the case of Mr. H. were very comprehensive. At the end of the therapy, he no longer had any psychosomatic panic attacks, did not suffer anymore from serious depressive crises and self-doubts, and with regard to his appearance had developed from a thick podge to a handsome man of normal weight. In his job, he appeared more successful

and was respected by his students, which had hardly before been the case because of his weak self-assertion. The father had come to the point where he invited Mr. H. still only as a visitor to a rooming house, but the patient hardly wanted to accept this in the end.

With regard to the communication with his wife, he managed to acquire more adult forms of communication. At the end of the therapy, the couple had the baby they had longed for, and moved into a larger and nicer apartment. The couple's circle of friends has also been changed in their favor.

The therapy figures accompanying the therapy process are shown in the appendix under the name of the case example (see appendix 4.2).

Therapeutic Summary of the Long-Term Case Example of the Patient Detlef Heinel:
From my point of view, the result of the long-term development of the above-mentioned therapy is very comprehensive and positive. The patient had done all stages of a structural universal psychotherapy with a high degree of self-commitment and had in many stages been able to use in a fertile way the therapy objects offered as transitional transference objects. Within the framework of the therapeutic relationship work, the objects used – ranging from large objects to stuffed animals – were able to enhance a purposeful illustration of the structures of a psychic disorder, of the emotional state, or of the interpersonal perception, and to support a change of the relationship structures in terms of trial actions. Another effect of the use of the therapy objects was that the patient was also made aware of new – so far unconscious – disorder issues in a gentle way for the relationship and made obvious to the patient in slow motion steps. For the therapist too they provided a good opportunity of working both *in and on the transference* in a continuous therapeutic process.

By deepening his self-knowledge on the basis of trial actions and thanks to parallel, more consistent detachment procedures, I think that to some extent it had been easier for the patient to fully utilize the possibilities of conceptual differentiation than it would have been feasible on the basis of a mere human confrontation.

In addition, the performance provided a good opportunity for seeking new problem solutions in specific activity structures on the basis of self-experiments.

2.2 Case Examples of Using Objects in Group Therapy

In connection with our approach of a structural universal group psychotherapy, some parallel examples of the concept of a course group and of the concept of a closed group should actually also always be presented (see above under 1.3.5 and 1.4). But except for some comparative comments, I would like to refer only to presentations of cases of closed groups, because the special procedure is more impressive for the patients here, but also more difficult to deal with for the therapists.

In view of the fact that the procedure is designed more educationally and introductorily for the group participants, the group atmosphere will be less relationship-dynamic for the patients, thus providing a helpful setting for new clients and heavily traumatized clients. But due to the stronger transference and introject processes in closed groups led by a mediator, the disorder to be worked on dynamically becomes processable in new social communities more in-depth in terms of the underlying cause and wider in terms of the range of the clients' independent solution-specific resources. The therapy objects used will usually be better "beseelt" according to the level of the atmosphere in the group and used in terms of a higher quality of the vaguely associatively and emotionally laden impression than would be possible in an individual therapy.

2.2.1 Case Examples of Establishing Contact and of Changing the Setting in the Therapy Group

At the beginning of a course group as well as at the beginning of a therapy unit of two and a half days of a closed group, the patients first have to introduce themselves with respect to their emotional state, their concern, their expectations, and their fears. Here, as in every form of group therapy, it is a general rule that each participant has to enter into a minimum verbal contact and to provide a minimal transparency regarding the disorder which is to be worked on.

As therapists we try to adequately clarify any basic disorders or misinterpretations with regard to the therapy work in advance, in one or more individual conversations. So the patients have already come to know a number of therapy objects in connection with the establishment of a contact in their relationship to the therapist in the course of their individual therapies. And in the same way they have experienced a strengthening of their resources due to these objects, and they have made their first steps in a focus-oriented work on the disorder by including these "beseelbare" objects.

This is important, because in general a certain autonomous regression process will be launched at first due to the mere setting of a group, so that at the beginning the participants will again lose something of their independent therapeutic competence to work on their problem. The level of the transference will then frequently be transferred by the patient to the disorder level in his or her family, with the result that the patient will act more dependent and/or more vigorous in the community. This, of course, is also a great opportunity for working on the disorder in a complex and reality-nearer way, as it often corresponds with actually experienced (family-related) relationship influences.

In the case of course groups, we quickly take on leadership as (parental) therapists, as expected of us, and suggest that the group do some warming up exercises of a body therapeutic nature; this quickly has a relaxing effect on the group. Ball games to learn the others' names or gymnastics exercises coupled with a mutual introduction of the participants are also important in this connection, among other things.

That means that simple contact exercises have a tension-reducing and a group coherence-enhancing effect in a movement setting.

This is different in closed groups. Here, the group participants refer more specifically to each other, and based on our previous work experience I would say, also to the group therapists. After a little general warming up and the presentation of the individual status of self-experience the aim is to comprehend also dynamically the current level of group, in order to be able to create later a common, favorable working atmosphere.

According to our experience, there are some recurring patterns, which are then brought into the movement picture by means of the therapy objects. For one, old questions of confidence are raised again, because the common feeling of a community among the group participants in cooperation with the therapists has got lost a bit since the last therapy unit ten or twelve weeks ago. Besides this re-affirmation of the group's coherence, old and new competitions are dynamically to be noted as a new fight about the structure of the group. If such problems are the dominating contact-specific subject, we – or the group itself, usually in the form of mediators – propose to use the big group rope as a movement therapeutic change of the setting.

As for the order, we determine, that the aggressive part is to be carried out first and then the harmonizing part. The rules that nobody will be allowed to injure himself or herself or anybody else physically are reiterated in advance within the framework of a verbal agreement. Thereafter, each group participant looks for a place at the big ring rope according to his or her sympathy, and then the literally increasing pulling begins. Everybody is pulling with their full strength or together with their coalition partners in one or the other direction.

If the participants are exhausted, or if they experience any changing feelings of solidarity, they will successively exchange their positions at the ring rope in order try other coalition partners. It usually does not take more than ten minutes until the first fears of contact and order of ranking aggressions have been overcome. After this joint work, the group appears to be more alert – and the individual more relaxed.

Then, in the second hold-testing part of the exercise, all group participants stand around the ring rope and hold it with both hands like in the case of the holding rocker (see above, case example of Sven Reimann in 2.1.2), while letting themselves fall backwards, more or less, depending on their respective degree of fear. Everybody lets himself fall back only so far that he will still be able to catch himself in the case of an emergency – but at the same time far enough that he consciously makes his contribution to the (regressive) balance of the group. In the case of advanced groups, there will usually still be a third exercise part, where all participants stand in the closed ring of the rope, letting themselves still more courageously fall back with their hips into the group's rope.

Then all patients are asked by the two therapists, if necessary, to now look calmly into the eyes of the other group participants and to try to sense which physical resonance they feel with each participant. Thereafter, the contact exercise will be evaluated verbally while sitting in a circle on chairs.

Contact exercises may, of course, also be organized as a couple exercise or as a special exercise between a patient and a therapist, depending on whether there are any corresponding indications for a very individual contact problem. As in an individual therapy, contact sticks, gymnastics balls, hoops, or the small ring rope are used to that end.

Usually, however, group initiatives, because they strive for the joint establishment of relationships, are to be preferred to such individual actions.

Therapeutic Summary of the Use of Contact Exercises in a Group:
Depending on the dynamic level, the contact objects used in the group will become more or less transmitters of interpersonal relationship tensions and needs. The therapy objects will be used, if the *basic group atmosphere has been verbally specified* and if a joint resolution is strived for by the group participants.

The performance example of the group rope shows impressively that the perceived tensions will be given a body therapeutic room, while individual needs such as wanting to "seize" something can well be included in one and the same performance into a conscious activity picture as the simultaneous need of wanting „to be in a reliable relationship". The group participants can practically demonstrate their strength and solidarity to themselves and to each other, which to some extent has a more enhancing effect on the relationship than any verbal proclamation. At the same time, this joint action has the effect that the group immerses into a conscious regressive atmosphere, which can be reinforced by each one individually and which can be modified by a spontaneous exchange of partners. These spontaneous experiments and the readiness to accept the slight alienation of the social contact interaction are at the same time the basis for training conditions, which will later be necessary for the "beseelte" use of objects and for translating inner psychic conflict constellations into external interactional activity-specific performances.

In a hypothetical interpretation, the thick group rope is to be considered as an objectified relationship framework of the therapists, because they must pay special attention to a balanced relationship between individuality and community and thus help to organize the "ring rope atmosphere" of the group.

2.2.2 Case Examples of Strengthening Resources in the Introductory Phase of Therapy

If the group has reached the level of an adequate contact among each other, the aim – as in an individual therapy – will be to create little manageable stress tests, so as to call upon the group's own resources to find solutions, and to gradually create in coordination with the therapists a good therapeutic working atmosphere.

Within the dynamics of a closed group, we additionally aim at directing the dependency wishes of the individual participants more towards the group's solidarity in terms of a solution and at training the therapeutic leadership power of the mediators of the group who are to be selected, on the basis of manageable dynamic sections of 90 minutes. This selection of the mediator couple will be supported by us as the therapist couple so clearly so that always the patient couple will or should be selected for the respective section of 90 minutes, who at the moment obviously represents the most advanced self-experience aspects in the group. They should both be able to focus on their own therapeutic concern and to show a perception ranging wide enough for a balanced group process.

We think that this differentiation process already has a resource-strengthening effect, since important competences of the individual group participants will be enhanced here by the capacity for regression in a combination with progression. The criteria for regression and progression abilities which will be clearly emphasized by the therapist couple help to make any therapeutic relationship and treatment structures transparent and comprehensible, which is an important prerequisite for the evaluation of structural activity-specific performances.

Without this dynamic basic knowledge of one's own and the others' psychic state, including the group dynamic transference and introject patterns, any conceptual orientation in the group will fail. If only the loudest, most aggressive, most depressive, or most mysterious participant of the group carries his or her point, structural activity-specific performances may also lead to acting out in the group. Structural activity-specific performances may, as a principle, not be more successful than is possible on the basis of the dynamic level of the group being enhanced by the respective mediators or by the actively supervising therapists.

No mediators will be selected in the course groups, as mentioned before, so that more individual conflicts will come to bear in the relationship to us as therapists. The clarifications of the relationships in the closed group will lead to more common development steps due to the mediators' work, which in turn will usually lead again to renewed (short) detachment from the mother and the father or the respective reference persons.

To symbolize these interaction barriers specified previously in the group, the black giant limp bag and the red giant block (see appendix 4.1) have always been selected so far. The movement psychotherapeutic release of any disappointments, frustrations, physical violence suffered, and any authoritarian intimidations takes place in individual actions with hands and feet in the supporting circle of the group or as a shared action in a small or team group. In the case of a high degree of solidarity-based action-specific activities in the community, especially, the emotional associations in the group will be very strengthening.

In one evaluation round, somebody once said that he felt that the joint action released something archaic in terms of power and strength, as if a primeval herd of hunters were killing an extremely strong mammoth. I think this image is in so far absolutely right in that it is true that the individual releases more reserves of strength in a coordinated group action than in the individual therapies before.

If these or other group movement actions aiming at a reciprocal effect have encouraged the participants enough to express any feelings, then the mutual safety experience will at the same time also have grown for the individual, since this individual has vividly experienced spontaneous expressions of actions on the part of the other participants with a temporary reinforcement and a subsequent withdrawal.

Resource-oriented performances are not only practiced in the beginning phase of the formation of the group, but also repeatedly and spontaneously

– later in a more casual form – as a kind of emotional recovery after strenuous self-experience performances of the participants, because then there is always an increased need to experience closeness. In such moments, such resource-oriented performances include, for example, building a *group's hut out of all available objects*, playing a *group animal zoo with self-selected stuffed animals* on the floor, or an action-filled organization of a *group birthday party with various "artistic contributions"* from all participants. Usually, such initiatives are a lot of fun, and thus they help to deal with any further painful or shameful psychic downs in the next round.

Therapeutic Summary of the Use of Resource-Oriented Performances in the Group:
The strengthening of resources in the group is important for stabilizing the individual and for the group members' getting to know each other on a dynamic basis.

Within the concept of a course group, the therapists may weigh to what extent the patients in the group will be in a position to work in a relatively uninhibited atmosphere and also to engage the other clients to help in connection with the structures to be worked on. These minimum qualities relating to conscious regression and progression abilities will be established more systematically in a closed group – under the special consideration of some dynamic points of view. In the resource-oriented phase, the mediators will also be specifically selected and trained in terms of their activity-specific competences.

Therefore, the transference mechanisms with regard to symbolizing objects are more important for establishing a group coherence. By dealing actively activity-specifically and with solidarity with the transitional transference objects for the mother and the father (or the corresponding transference persons), the group's joint reserve of strength will be strengthened, the taboo will be removed from the old (parents) and the new (therapists) transference figures, and thereby the status of the mediators as the leaders of the confrontative actions will also be raised.

After a successful strengthening of resources, the level of any focus-oriented individual work will therefore be qualitatively better in the therapeutic team, and the working atmosphere will be more trustful than prior to this developmental stage. Furthermore, such resource-oriented work also serves the purpose of psychic regeneration and fulfilling the needs for coherence after any exhausting self-experience processes.

2.2.3 Case Examples of Focus-Related Work with a Therapeutic Team in the Group

The structural activity-specific performances relating to the work on a focus are done by the patients in therapeutic teams, which are put together by the clients according to their own notions or based on the result of a discussion about the performance in the group.

Each patient may suggest a subject of his or her own to be worked on, according to his or her current rational clarity, emotional self-resonance, and motivational state of need. In this connection, the patient is asked to specify the presumable aim of the performance, to substantiate the reasons for doing so, and to explain why this subject is currently – in the reality of the external world and in this situation of the group – of relevance to him or her. Thereafter, the patient can describe and propose the setting of the performance – including the patients selected for cooperation in the performance -, or release it for a free association in the group. The group, the respective mediators, and the therapists will then discuss the pro's and con's of the proposed setting or of a setting still to be sought. Depending on the dynamic level of the group, previous experiences with the patient, or any momentary relevance of the therapy framework in the patient's currently experienced behavior situation, will also be included in the discussion.

A setting is considered to have been created in a therapy enhancing way, once the patient who is interested on working on a subject has either designed or assumed a structural activity-specific performance, to which to majority of the group members – including the mediators and therapists – has given their agreement, because they can see therein a certain diagnostic sense or a solution-oriented chance of development.

Sometimes, destructive transferences which have not been sufficiently perceived or subliminal negative introjects lead to a "heavy repetitive stagnation" of the unresolved conflict, to a compulsory re-traumatization of the previously damaged child, or to a problem theme of only secondary or tertiary importance, in order to divert from a more important psycho-dynamic connection. A few specific comments will be made to this in the following long-term case examples (see 2.2.4).

Once the setting has been relatively suitably chosen, the patients who are to participate in the performance, will be determined next both by the individual and the group, as well as by the coordinators. This therapeutic team in its closer sense also includes the roles of the supporter and of someone for the patient to hold on to in the setting. The supporter has to challenge the active behaviour of the performing patient. The person to hold on to has to support the patient during – and especially after – the therapeutic performance actively with words or physical attention and care.

After the activity-specific performance or a performance section of two or three patients, we again talk in the large group, while sitting on chairs in a circle, about what the patients experienced and whether or not the result is compatible with the objective stipulated before. Thereafter, the whole group discusses again the setting on the basis of a pre-/post-comparison as well as any additional observations, evaluation-specific feelings, and problem-specific interpretations, concerning both the participants actively involved and those not actively involved.

2.2.4 Long-Term Group Development in Structural Universal Group Psychotherapy

The closed group described here worked together for two years. It had been structured according to the concept outlined above in 1.3.5 (see above) and met once in a quarter for a total of eight therapy events. In addition to the group therapy, all the participants had individual therapy sessions with my wife or with me.

According to the structure of a universal group psychotherapy as outlined in this book, activity-specific performances are to be distinguished from such performances which aim at establishing a contact or at strengthening resources, or which belong to the regular experimental focus-oriented work. Similar to the long-term case development described in 2.1.5 (see above), the performance concepts which were specifically effective or consciously used by the respective participants will be outlined and substantiated in a summarized form as a representation of the whole case. If possible or required, I will also try to outline the therapeutic assessment of the group dynamic situation being required for the indication of the performance, so that the direction principles of the mediators or our attitudes as therapists can be made transparent.

The Contact Performances of the Long-Term Group "Twelve" *:
During five out of the total of eight therapy events of the closed group Twelve, the group rope was used in the contact phase of the patients' encounter, both to express any diverging tensions in the group and to symbolize the support of the group. In the course of these five uses of the rope, a trend toward a transition was to be noted, from a previously more power-stressed fight between two groups and subgroups to a commonly experienced swinging, resembling a compromise. (The setting of the group rope has been described

in 2.2.1 – see above.)

During the process of the therapy performances, the patients often changed their places and orientations at the group rope, so as to be able to feel again the solidarity of another group member or also to experience other group participants as fighting opponents. But that meant also that the relationship structures were experimentally increasingly loosened, and this in turn led to the development of less rigid coalition liaisons.

Following the group rope, the nonverbal welcome rituals and group-specific warming up exercises of the individual participants played an important role in the contact phase. Usually, the group was standing or moving in a circle, and each member had the task – in an optional order – to present a movement or expression exercise to the group, which was then performed by all.

Among the ideas which generated a lot of fun and were very popular were the "group animal zoo" and "the novel sports session". When doing these exercises, the patients often regressed to the level of school children or of a nursery and lost their social contact inhibitions. The bodily movements led almost incidentally to spontaneous body contacts and to a funny alienation of communication rituals.

This tension-releasing relationship behaviour was usually set against the very dynamic interactions aiming at clarifying the relationship, which took place at the beginning of all group therapy days in the "chair rounds". There, the participants were asked to explain again in a credible way their therapy concerns and report about the impacts of the changes in their external reality, which they had announced last before the group. It was typical that quite a number of contradictions were usually hidden in these summaries, and that reproaches were only directed towards external causers. At the same time, the autonomous work of the mediators also kept some confusing relationship traces in the meanwhile small and large groups, which we, as the main therapists then had to investigate.

All that means that one again comes into contact with the emotional resonance framework of one's own disorder, and that one has to be ready to engage in the atmospherically labilizing milieu of the opening of the resistance in favor of new growth demands and development chances.

Especially during this contact phase, "the prices were stipulated", which would later be the basis of the serious context analysis in connection with the work on the disorder of the individual members, and which were decisive for the question of how cooperative the next work would be done.

As therapists, we experienced the group as relatively balanced in terms of the ratio of power of the individual members, both with respect to the group and the genders among each other.

During the dynamic phase focussing on the establishment of the readiness to work, the group was forced again and again at the beginning to clarify residues of any "old parental authority conflicts" and to re-experience that more regression and progression space comes into being in a "cooperative large family" than any individual would be able to organize. For this reason, we prevented in this phase any premature focus-oriented work (which we, in contrast, usually enhance early in far less dynamic course groups), because it is necessary to have more conceptual similarity in the group in terms of the perception and the therapeutic assessment of results, as a basis for the forthcoming psychic stress both in a good and in a difficult sense, in order to ensure a good quality of work.

Therapeutic Summary of the Contact Performances with the Long-Term Group Twelve:

The patient group tested and strengthened a lot of creative relationship ability during the contact performances. At the beginning, symbolizations were established where the dynamic ambivalence conflicts of the wish for individual regard could be performed by means of objects, while at the same time being reliably held with the group rope. At the emotional culminating point of the individual or coalition-controlled fight versus the longing for a trustful giving and taking of holding functions, this closed rope became the transitional transference object of shared and contradictory concerns. The group rope also represented, however, the connecting framework we provided as structure-enhancing therapists. Our dynamic contributions as the main therapists (and later active supervisors) led to clarifying orientations in the emotional milieu of the group in terms of a serious as well as playful establishment of a relationship.

The purpose of this was to enhance a shared conceptuality in activity-specific structures with the aim of opening up new trial fields for later changes of the external reality in the behavior of the individual.

Resource-Oriented Performances of the Long-Term Group Twelve:

Movement and conversation initiatives in the phase of strengthening of emotional reserves and of creative potencies are often inseparably connected with the contact performances, as also described in the long-term case example of Detlef Heinel (see above under 2.1.5). The only difference is that the emotional negative dynamic aspect of the patients' therapy identity has already faded away in so far as they are already on their way to developing their ability to work, and the important points in the basic foundations of the therapeutic reflection and assessment ability have already been laid.

That means that resource-oriented performances in the group tend to enhance once again consciously the reliable framework of the patient/therapist relationships and test the regression and progression capacity of the individual. And this is achieved without pursuing the difficult individual focuses of a disorder or allowing any such pursuits on the part of the respective leaders (mediators and/or main therapists). Thereby any re-traumatization dangers due to untested group relationships can also be better avoided.

Usually, the black giant limp bag and, if necessary, also the red giant block were used for a resource-oriented release of tension in the group after the emotional verbal turning point when dealing with a conflict in the group.

In seven of eight meetings of the group, these large symbolizing objects were included at least once during the first sessions of the group therapy event in an aggression-releasing and relationship-enhancing way. Basically, it was clear to the group members each time that the point could not anymore be the mere anger at any deprivations, disappointments, and violence suffered, etc., but that an important aim of the performance was the wish to participate in and to let others participate in strong emotions of the community. Everybody demonstrated in how far he or she was able to engage himself or herself with strong affects and to control them again within a few seconds.

This "body certifying" training of regressions on the one hand and of progressive observation and control possibilities on the other hand is a verbally irreplaceable behavioral line of evidence in the group process. In the course of any mostly aggressive presentation of "change-specific energies", there was often a spontaneous formation of small groups which acted on the symbolizing objects in a rhythmic or an orderly and expressive simultaneous way. As of about the fourth group event, it became an almost fixed group ritual for the whole group to lift the black giant bag at the end and then drop it to the floor at top speed. Above I already once spoke of (see under 2.1.5) "killing the mammoth of a primeval herd" as a comparison with the archaic. The group members taking the lead here are usually also those leading in the process of developing a community capable of withstanding strain.

Besides these standards, the group Twelve used all possible movement performances, which in the framework of the repetitive character of the group development also became strengthening rituals. This group took a special pleasure in loud sounds, vigorous stamping, and circle exercises with their hands, while running forward and backward. These proven resource exercises were also used for a re-orientation of progressive powers in situations where the group was in a very sad mood.

In the course of the group events gentle performances were also done

143

relating to individuals' holidays, or where laudable properties of the group members were consciously presented, or where an appreciation of one's self-esteem was distinctly expressed as model actions in terms of resource-oriented performances in the group process.

Therapeutic Summary of the Resource Performances of the Long-Term Group Twelve:
After an often quite dynamic beginning, the patient group usually found a movement therapeutic form to enhance the resources of its individual members as well as of the group as a whole. Such resource-enhancing interventions were often triggered by joint actions on the basis of a shared identification towards external threats or jointly-diagnosed introjects of their own (in the advanced group process).

The joint practicing and finding of predictable communication rituals obviously have a strengthening effect for many group members. The mutually testifying experience of regression and progression potencies also has an identity-enhancing effect. In this context, model actions are experienced as with older siblings, confirmation as with good parents, or imitation as with curious children. All this helps to establish a reliable perception-specific and conceptual evaluation atmosphere, which helps to practice joint actions in the form of a "psychic first aid" in an experienceable way for all group members.

The Focus-Oriented Performances of the Long-Term Group Twelve:
Working in therapeutic teams is the main performance method used in long-term groups. As described above in 2.1.3 and 2.1.4, each group member first presents to the whole group a subject which is to be worked on. The subject proposed will then be discussed and thus further tested with respect to its therapy relevance, and modified in terms of a challenging compromise for the individual, or supported. At the end of this discussion, the confrontative, supporting and/or the team for holding the patient is formed for each patient; in principle, the two group therapists may also be included in these teams.

The focuses announced in this context by the individual group members are a reciprocal product of the individual subject-related preparation of the individual and the group dynamic stimulation of the subject in the current experience of the patient. Against this background it is generally comprehensible that the proposed work-specific focuses of the first therapy rounds dealt with the individuals' regulation of closeness and distance, their basic problems with establishing boundaries and their basic authority problems with their parents, as well as conflicts relating to their siblings. Settings in terms of family constellations with sculptures (objects such as stuffed animals) and for expressing and working on transferences such as with the black giant bag and red giant block were a favourite choice. In addition to these clarifying and tension-releasing performances, there was a slight transition from the "beseelbare" objects to exercises with the real therapists in manifold positive as well as negative transference forms starting at the end of the second group event.

For the majority of the group's patients it was important, for example, that it was possible to hurl even the emotionally most negative transference at us (e.g. by kicking the black bag) or hit us over the head with arguments (e.g. hitting with the club on the block or bag) in a combined setting with the objects, so as to not only be complaining about built-up anger with respect to the reference persons. The confidence which in the meantime had grown towards us as the main therapists, opened the way for performances relating to true closeness with us, where small sequences with and without any object (imitation of football, stuffed animal dialogues, holding rocker, etc.) were used especially often to work on any such issues.

During meetings in the middle phase of the therapy, the group developed the uniform wish to show us as their better parents once their true milieu of origin and to look together with us for new paths of development. After assuming a negative parental role figure, each patient then represented a scene from his or her family, using therapy objects. Then each patient tried to support himself or herself consoling through self-acceptance. Yet, most patients succeeded in doing this only by means of a stuffed animal and with the help of a prompting coach. Finally, a performance with better parents was developed, and we were often spontaneously invited or requested to do this. For some clients such a performance was planned, while for others it was experimentally and spontaneously developed in a focus-oriented way.

Almost exactly in the middle of the overall therapy time, most patients had chosen early and shameful repressed subjects to work on as a focus of the group treatment.

Four female patients' situations were dealing with repetitive sexual abuse. In the case of four other patients and of a multi-traumatized woman, family-related subjects of considerable physical violence had to be worked out.

In addition, there were three female patients who had a dissociate disorder of a well limited or medium degree within a multi-diagnosis. The underlying, very central negative childhood experiences were worked on and discussed one after the other in teams in a focus-oriented way almost only by means of transitional transference objects in the form a group setting, because nobody wanted or was able to assume the role of any perpetrators of such seriousness. Working on the subjects in conversation rounds was again and again essential because of the integrating effect – but strong anxieties and affects also had to be released by activity-specific performances. The actual situations of abuse or violence were not represented in this connection. They had been worked on before in an individual therapy with the help of a screening or EMDR setting.

In the group rounds it was important that the perpetrators were both individually and jointly ostracized so that the patients could have the feeling of being rehabilitated in the community again or for the first time. In the later part of the focus-oriented group work, role plays on introject transference and introject generation structures were increasingly the content-specific focuses of the team work, where the point was less diagnostic but rather solution-oriented issues. But many of the focus-oriented subjects became "experimental by themselves" during the specific actual performance, because the awakening of creative resources could no longer be stopped in view of any setting agreement within the framework of a benevolent group dynamic.

Therapeutic Summary of the Focus-Oriented Performances of the Long-Term Group Twelve:
In the course of its therapy the patient group described had created important self-experience structures in teams based on subject-focused activity-specific performances. It has to be emphasized that the group grew dynamically closer together, and that aspects of solidarity were essential for the emergence of difficult and most difficult treatment focuses, which wouldn't have happened in the case of a cooler relationship atmosphere.

The use of "beseelbare" transference objects in this context was helpful to symbolize the presence of detestable perpetrators, which could be used in this object form to deal with the conflict – and thus for a gradual liberation and the establishment of boundaries. By practicing "beseelbare" structures, the danger of a re-traumatization is reduced at the same time, because patients were given the opportunity of psycho-dynamically practicing their own regulation of affects at the distance they wanted to observe, and so they also gained more sureness in their external reality with respect to any potential perpetrators.

In an atmosphrere of mutual regard and showing solidarity in cooperation, the focuses proposed for a therapeutic performance become increasingly more variable and experimental, so that the therapeutic group process gets going quite automatically in a phase where structures already exist.

Experimental Focus-Oriented Performances of the Long-Term Group Twelve:

In the above description of the therapy development of the patient group all major aspects of the experimental alignment of work have basically already been indicated.

An experimental procedure can be chosen from the beginning of a therapy up to the end of a therapeutic treatment. It depends on the interpersonal level of the group, the relationship to the therapists, and the progress of the patients with regard to their structural adoption capacity. But in addition to the experimental chance of sometimes only a few minutes, the unpredictable dynamic chaos or the patient's lack of structure also have to be considered a therapeutic danger in this context.

The above-mentioned group of patients created the prerequisites for a qualitatively good – experimentally mature – working atmosphere by consciously working through the dynamic relationship process and by practicing the structures relating thereto in the roles of the mediators, as well as by individual work in small teams. This was, of course, accompanied by the usual fluctuations of individual members and the typical "3-day development" of the group as a well-known resistance procedure of different degree.

While making music with Orffian instruments was still the possible positive culminating point of the experimental focus-oriented work in the sense of searching for resonance during the first round of the group therapy, already in the third round of the therapy the theme of a common relationship structure based on a division of work was allotted space through the building of a common hut for the group. After positive experiments in the community, the individual was then also increasingly regarded and respected within the experimental performance work of a self-selected team.

Before, however, the priority was given to an open research of the setting with the therapists – at least in the form of contact and resource-oriented activity-specific performances. The culminating point of the first part of the treatment of the group was then that a number of the patients could use the therapists as positive substitutes for their parents in role play scenes, without predetermining the structure of the plot. These patients just wanted to experience us as substitute parents – to some extent they wanted to experience in a modelled play, and to some extent also in real roles, how we might satisfy the needs of "the not yet fully adult children". The acceptance of any spontaneous affection during the performance of lovely scenes with little children before the eyes of the (protecting) group, was an experimental and solution-oriented part of a trial experience in this connection, which helped to develop new structures.

In addition, increasingly more fellow patients tended to be included in the performances than at the beginning. The purpose of this was that "new siblings should also contribute to better experiences in the life of the family", and based on past experiences, one could trust the majority of the group members.

After there had been closeness exercises with the therapists during the first third of the therapy, a number of the patients of the group Twelve developed in the last third of the treatment a need to have a chance of tussling with their "substitute parents" and of touching them directly. That meant, for example, competing in strength with ropes, bags or blocks or in an infantile contact with stuffed animals. After the long start-up phase, other group participants also dared to engage in intensive physical touches in front of the group. For instance, some of them wanted to be well-cared for by us while lying in the hammock, touched with our hands, and to be looked at close up with a clear gaze.

Others preferred the hover belt for experiments with being carried and swinging, which they hadn't done so far. After stopping, we usually held the patients carefully by the head and neck in their regressive roles of little children.

The patients of the group Twelve looked for confirmation as juveniles going through puberty and adults through reality-related inquiries to us as fellow citizens or as a couple during the discussions of the group.

The final status of the group in terms of the experimental focussing was that we had invested a lot of time and efforts in working on acting introjects to which we are possibly more exposed to as adults than to any infantile transferences. But in this respect, the therapy status of the group remained uncompleted. Important questions of individual, partnership-related or social identity and as conscious, politically-thinking citizens of a country could also only be touched on superficially in view of the short time of the therapy.

Therapeutic Summary of the Experimental Performances of the Long-Term Group Twelve:
In the course of their therapy, the patients' group Twelve slowly changed from a firmly structured to an experimentally outlined focus-oriented work.

A prerequisite for such a qualitative inclusion of intuitions on a larger scale are individual emotional perception and evaluation structures on the part of the group participants as well as a common deepening of a progressive group dynamic which is transparent for the majority and which also has to be controlled by the individual participants.

Along with diagnostic analyses of any unclear disorder context, the search for new solution structures for so far little-known or unknown relationship patterns is a great opportunity within such an experimental framework.

On the one hand, such a work challenges resources responding to the autonomous self-healing competence. On the other hand, experimental settings are also organized by clients, when they are prepared to learn intensively from others or to test their behavior as an orientation model.

At the end of an experimental relationship development, the relationships between the patient and the therapist tend to become increasingly more reality-related and more authentic compared to the adult life environments of everybody else.

Here too, clients must have structural performance platforms for adult encounter spaces in which then all symbolizing objects will be superfluous or only be diverting, because now the real-life models of the therapists and the patients are requested. But the therapists are also asked to drop any indulgence towards the patients in order to give them a chance of being equal by confronting them with direct criticism of their adult weaknesses and contradictions, and to give them a chance to accumulate experiences in a shorter period of time.

In this sense, the motivated long-term patient will at the end of an experimental psychotherapeutic relationship work come up with his or her questions at just that point where the therapist is able to be at that moment. The aim is, however, not an assimilation of the images of both but that each one learns how to find his or her individual solution and to advocate it with respect to his or her quality of life and morality.

In this evaluation of the whole therapy it had to be noted that on the one hand important developmental steps got going on the part of each group member, but that on the other hand the individual quality of life and adult morality of the participants of this self-experience group are very differently accentuated from our point of view (as older partners of this community) and that to some extent, more time would still have been required to work on parental introjects.

3 Present Results and Research of Effects within the Framework of the Practice of Structural Universal Psychotherapy

3.1 Presentation and Description of Results in Individual and Group Therapy on the Basis of Statistical Computations and Categorial Evaluations

a) On the structure of the random sample investigated

These statistical computations are a first attempt to get a metric feedback to the therapeutic changes observed. Franke's BSI (Brief Symptom Inventory) questionnaire (2000) as described in 1.5 and the questionnaire regarding the patient's satisfaction, which I developed and am currently testing, were included to that end. This means that the majority of the statistical computations are of a descriptive nature. The random sample of the patients included from our joint practice in the last three to five years is relatively small, since only such patients could be included in the questionnaires regarding the patient's satisfaction who had done a universal psychotherapy of at least 100 sessions either with my wife or with me. The majority of these patients were also participants of the group psychotherapy described in 1.3.5, which was paid by the patients themselves.

About a quarter of the group therapy patients suffered from a psychotrauma; this was known to about half of the patients at the beginning of the therapy, and about half of the patients had not been aware of this problem so far. The latter only became aware of this traumatic correlation in the course of the advanced therapeutic work, where it then became obvious to these patients on the basis of scenes.

The diagnostic range of the main diagnoses weighted in connection with the random sample was as follows:

Table 12: Random sample of the patients included in the analyses of the patient's satisfaction

		Number	Percent
A	depressive anxiety neuroses	19	38,00 %
B	depressive obsessive-compulsive disorders	11	22,00 %
C	narcissistic neuroses	8	16,00 %
D	structural disorders	7	14,00 %
E	various personality disorders	5	10,00 %

Number = 50   Average age = 32.2 years   Gender-specific ratio: 52 % women, 48 % men

Within the framework of the therapy, the patients worked in the following therapy settings:

Table 13:

		Number	Percent
A	Closed therapy group in combination with an individual therapy	36	72,00 %
B	Open course groups only in combination with individual therapy	8	16,00 %
C	Individual psychotherapy treatments only	6	12,00 %
Z from A, B, C	Special psycho-trauma therapy in combination with individual and/or group psychotherapy	18	36,00 %

That means that the psychotrauma patients became acquainted with overlapping treatment offers. This list of special questions was still taken into consideration, because we wanted to investigate trends of differences in the results of the treatment with regard to combinations of settings.

b) On the evaluation of the BSI (Brief Symptom Inventory)

The BSI questionnaires of a total of 131 test persons were evaluated. Included in the total number of these test persons were: First, individuals who were originally interested in a therapy and completed the questionnaire, but who then cancelled their registration during the time they had to wait for a therapy (pre-1 variable). Second, we received questionnaires from patients, who are presently still waiting for a therapy (pre-1 variable). Third, we received questionnaires from patients, who started a therapy (pre-2 variable with a test 6 months in advance). Fourth, we had the BSI completed by patients doing a therapy after the 100th session (post-1 variable).

A review of the symptom check list led to the following results:

Table 14: Group waiting for a therapy versus therapy group

	N	M	SD
BSI pre-1 variable only	50	2.35	0.77
BSI post-1 variable only	51	2.04	0.60

Statistics for review: T99 = 2.49; p < 0.05 significant for a comparison of the therapy groups (T – Test for independent random samples with regard to the total score of the BSI)

Table 15: Group waiting for a therapy at the time of registration versus group at the beginning of the treatment after having waited for a therapy

	N	M	SD
BSI pre-1 variable	30	2.11	0.60
BSI post-1 variable	30	2.06	0.55

Statistics for review: T29 = 0.71; p = 0.48 not significant for a control group comparison (T – Test for independent random samples with regard to the total score of the BSI)

These results reveal the tendency that the result of non-treated patients is significantly worse according to the BSI than the result of treated patients, which might indicate the relief of symptoms. But since the random samples included in the upper chart are not dependent, these assessments may only be interpreted to a limited extent. The results for the same patients based on a pre/post-comparison will be available in one to two years.

Yet, when the control group comparison is included, then the assumption of a positive influence of the treatment will again be supported, since no significant changes of the emotional state of the patients were obvious when comparing the questionnaires of the group waiting for a therapy and the group at the beginning of the treatment after having waited for a therapy, i.e. between pre-1 and pre-2 variable.

c) Evaluation of the questionnaire regarding the patient's satisfaction
Category: Sick days – visits to the doctor

1. Number of sick days per year, prior to and after the therapy:

Graph 9:

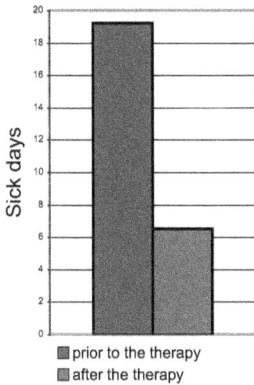

Number = 50
T49=2.57; p<0.05 (significant)
Sick days reported by the patients:
• prior to the therapy: 19.20 (SD 31.90)
• after the therapy: 6.54 (SD 18.63)

This means that the days the patients were certified as ill had decreased by about two thirds at the end of the therapy than before the beginning of the therapy, according to the patients' own statements. For objectivity purposes it would, however, have been even better, if this survey had been made separately prior to the beginning of the therapy and after the end of the therapy. But the tendency is still definitely positive, and this is sustainably supported by our empirical impressions.

2. List of the groups of doctors mentioned and visits to a doctor per year:

Table16:

N=50

Groups of doctors (categories)	Number of the groups of doctors visited prior to the therapy			Number of the groups of doctors visited after the therapy		
	first statement	second statement	third statement	first statement	second statement	third statement
No visit to a doctor	8 (16 %)	19	32	21 (42 %)	36	46
General practitioner	27 (54 %)	6	3	17 (34 %)	0	0
Neurologist	4 (8 %)	6	3	3 (6 %)	2	0
Orthopedist	3 (6 %)	6	1	0	1	0
Gynecologist or urologist	3 (6 %)	6	3	3 (6 %)	4 (8 %)	0
Internist and cardiologist	2 (4 %)	2	5 (10 %)	3 (6 %)	0	1
Pneumologist	1 (2 %)	0	0	1 (2 %)	0	1
Dentist	0	1	3 (6 %)	1 (2 %)	3 (6 %)	0
Ophthalmologist	0	0	0	1 (2 %)	2 (4 %)	1
Otorhinolaryngologist	0	0	0	0	2 (4 %)	0
Dermatologist	1 (2 %)	3	1	0	0	0
Radiologist	1 (2 %)	1	0	0	0	0
Total	50	50	50	50	50	50

153

This graph shows that 16 % of the patients had not visited a doctor prior to the therapy, whereas 54 % consulted a general practitioner. These rates had changed up to the time after the therapy, when 42 % of the patients reported not to visit a doctor and 34 % reported to continue to consult, in particular, a general practitioner.

Two statistical comparisons are purposeful to illustrate the development:

Graph 10: Visits to a doctor (absolute) per year

Graph11: Visits to groups of doctors (in general)

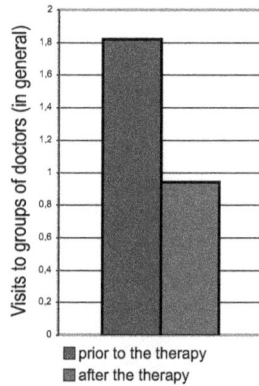

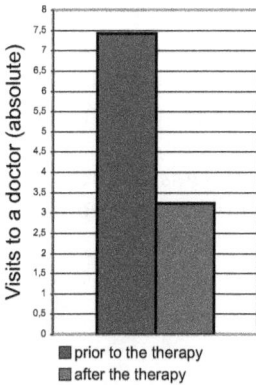

T49=4.01; N=50
p<0.001 (significant)
Visits to a doctor per year:
prior to the therapy: 7.42
after the therapy: 3.23

T49=6.47; N=50
p<0.001 (significant)
Average number of visits to groups of doctors:
prior to the therapy: 1.82
after the therapy: 0.94

This means that both the absolute number of visits to a doctor per year and the visits to groups of doctors decreased by about 50 %.

3. Frequency of visits to other medical specialists:

As for the question of visits to several medical specialists, there is a similar picture:

Table 17:

Number = 50

Time	No doctor	One specialist	Two specialists	Three specialists
Prior to the therapy	16 %	22 %	26 %	36 %
After the therapy	42 %	28 %	22 %	8 %

This means that not only the absolute number of visits to a doctor decreased but also the rate of visits to multiple medical specialists.

Unfortunately, no significant change could be noted when comparing the number of days the patients stayed in a hospital; but in view of only a few occasions, upon which our psychotherapy patients had to stay in a hospital, these facts are not very expressive and do not weigh very heavily.

A positive tendency in connection with visits to multiple medical specialists should, however, be mentioned, i.e. that the general practitioner played an increasingly central role, in view of the basis of the significantly reduced visits to a doctor.

Summarizing the results of this research it can be noted that a long-term psychotherapy of at least 100 sessions in the form of structural universal psychotherapy leads to a significant improvement of the individual's capability to work, i.e. of the individual's psycho-physical capability.

The reduction of the number of visits to a doctor and to other medical specialists indicates that healthier patients contribute noticeably to reductions in the treatment costs to be paid by their health insurance plan.

d) Evaluation of the questionnaire regarding the patient's satisfaction:
Category: Sub-questions in percent

The self-assessments regarding the sub-categories of the questions 1 to 7 were included in this analysis, but summarized in the satisfaction value for the purpose of an easy survey.

The descriptive statements regarding the patients' satisfaction indicate a general positive correlation with regard to the structural universal individual and group psychotherapy the patients underwent.

Table 18:

Number = 50

Question	Categories of satisfaction in percent					
	A) not satis- fied	B) partially satisfied	Sub-total resulting from A and B	C) satisfied	D) very satisfied	Sub-total resulting from C and D
	0 – 30 %	40 – 60 %		70 – 80 %	90 –100 %	
1a) generally satis- fied	2 %	20 %	22 %	56 %	22 %	78 %
1b) with therapy form	0 %	18 %	18 %	38 %	44 %	82 %
1c) with therapists	0 %	10 %	10 %	42 %	48 %	90 %
1d) with exercise opportunities	2 %	16 %	18 %	46 %	36 %	82 %
1e) with oneself	10 %	50 %	60 %	36 %	4 %	40 %
2) Change of one's personal value system	8 %	36 %	44 %	40 %	16 %	56 %
3) Change of health-conscious behaviour	16 %	38 %	52 %	38 %	10 %	48 %
4a) Work	20 %	36 %	56 %	34 %	10 %	44 %
4b) Social environ- ment	6 %	36 %	42 %	44 %	12 %	58 %
4c) Family	28 %	38 %	66 %	30 %	10 %	40 %
4d) Partnership	28 %	32 %	60 %	30 %	10 %	40 %
5a) Change at work	30 %	22 %	52 %	38 %	10 %	48 %
5b) Change in social environment	20 %	30 %	50 %	34 %	15 %	50 %
5c) Change in the family	14 %	34 %	48 %	46 %	16 %	62 %
6a) Your colleagues	18 %	42 %	60 %	30 %	10 %	40 %
6b) Your friends	24 %	26 %	50 %	32 %	18 %	50 %
6c) Your family	42 %	34 %	76 %	16 %	8 %	24 %
6d) Your partner	24 %	36 %	60 %	34 %	6 %	40 %
7a) Prior – work	26 %	48 %	74 %	20 %	6 %	36 %
7b) Prior – social environment	22 %	44 %	66 %	30 %	4 %	34 %
7c) Prior – family	22 %	42 %	64 %	24 %	12 %	36 %
7d) Prior - partner	36 %	46 %	82 %	10 %	8 %	18 %

It has to be noted that, according to their self-assessments, more than three quarters of the patients were satisfied with the therapy success in general, the therapy form, the therapists, and the exercise opportunities in model situations of the therapy. The patients were, however, only satisfied to a limited extent with their own commitment. The reason for such an assessment was usually, as we found out, the therapy chances the client had missed at the beginning of the therapy or in other resistance rounds.

The patients' personal value system and their health-conscious behavior had changed at least about 50 % according to the patients' self-assessments.

As therapists, we were at first a bit surprised when we found out that the *clients' present satisfaction* with regard to their colleagues, their social relationships, their family, and their partnership were only assessed as relatively satisfactory on average. When verifying the reasons for this upon inquiry, we learned that the patients' behavioural changes (as a result of the therapy) were not unrestrictedly welcomed by their environment, because these changes meant that habitual valuation patterns and reciprocal structures in the relationships had to be abandoned. In their environment, the patients' altered behavior found a mixed positive response. When comparing the results of questions 5 and 6 in terms of the structure of the answers, it becomes obvious that the patients tended to be more satisfied with their behavioral changes than were their environments and their relatives.

This contrast seems to be especially serious in the sub-item partnership. Here, the patients experienced important changes in their relationships, but at the same time, that their partners were apparently less satisfied or wanted to be less satisfied with the behavioral modifications they were now confronted with. To some extent, this is, however, also in line with our professional observations, in that the partnerships of psychotherapy patients are systematically embedded in disordered behavioral patterns and any healthier establishment of boundaries or any autonomous developments of the partner are often accompanied with "clinging worries" or with frustration because of the "neurotic loss of power". Here, the joint modification process obviously requires more time.

If one tries, however, to compare the satisfaction of the patient's environment according to the patient's assessment *prior to the therapy* with his or her assessment *after the therapy*, it has to be noted that especially in the case of the partnerships, there was a tendency of still more dissatisfaction *prior to the therapy*, so that the general modification tendency may still be considered as positive in the direction. Here, about two thirds of the reference persons concerned in the work, social, familial, and partnership environment were more dissatisfied with the patients before the therapy than after the therapy.

Altogether, I feel that the assessment of the patients themselves with regard to their therapeutic modification process should be more highly considered and more appreciated in terms of the general therapeutic success. Additional external criteria would, however, be considered desirable in further investigations for a holistic consideration of the therapeutic success.

e) Evaluation of the questionnaire regarding the patient's satisfaction:
Category: Therapy objects used

1. Therapy objects used as mentioned in all statements:

Table 19:

Number = 50

Cate-gory	Therapy Objects	1st statement		2nd statement		3rd statement		4th statement		5th statement	
		Number	%	Number	%	Number	%	Number	%	Number	%
A	Black giant bag	20	46,5 [1]	6	14,0 [2]	5	13,2 [2]	0	0	0	0
	Red giant block	1	2,2	3	7,0	3	7,9	3	13,6 [2]	1	5,9
	Clubs	2	4,3	3	7,0	1	2,6	1	4,5	0	0
	Harnesses	2	4,3	3	7,0	1	2,6	0	0	0	0
	Yellow bag	1	2,2	1	2,3	2	5,3	0	0	0	0
	Total	26	56,5	16	37,3	12	31,6	4	18,1	2	11,8
B	Giant tub	2	4,3	1	2,3	2	5,3	1	4,5	1	5,9
	Giant egg	1	2,2	0	0	2	5,3	0	0	1	5,9
	Mat	4	8,7 [3]	3	7,0	2	5,3	2	9,1	6	35,3 [1]
	Total	7	16,2	4	9,3	6	15,9	3	13,6	8	47,1
C	Stuffed animals	9	19,1 [1]	10	23,3 [1]	9	23,7 [1]	3	13,6 [2]	2	11,8 [2]
	Ropes	2	4,3	2	4,7	1	2,6	2	9,1	0	0
	Sticks	1	2,2	2	4,7	1	2,6	6	27,3 [1]	2	11,8 [2]
	Balls	0	0	0	0	0	0	2	9,1	0	0
	Total	12	25,6	14	32,7	11	28,9	13	59,1	4	23,6
D	Hammock	1	2,2	5	11,4 [3]	5	13,2 [2]	0	0	1	5,9
	Swing	0	0	2	4,7	1	2,6	0	0	1	5,9
	Total	1	2,2	7	16,3	6	15,8	0	0	2	11,8
Grand total		46	100	43	100	38	100	22	100	17	100

[ ] portion of a statement >10 %

(1)(2)(3) - position within a statement

Category A: primarily aggression objects
Category B: primarily special objects
Category C: primarily dialogue objects
Category D: primarily stabilization objects

This survey shows that especially the objects for negative transferences and for an aggressive expression of emotions are of greatest importance.

56 % of the patients with more than 100 therapy sessions of self-experience reported that they considered the elements of category A as very impor-

tant in their first statement to question 12.

In the second statement, at least two thirds were still of the opinion that high importance had to be attributed to these elements. Dialogue contact objects were in second place and up to the third statement increasingly considered to be beneficial.

They remain important for the entire therapy process.

From the third statement on, swinging objects and special objects were assessed as important. Of course, it might be objected that the specific offer of the symbolizing objects is also specifically aligned accordingly, so that the frequency of use would be suggested this way. But on the other hand it might also be possible that patients would come to a different subjective assessment. The question asked was specifically, which elements the patients experienced as helpful in which order. Thus the accent of the empirically assumed and available selection corresponds ultimately also with the tendency of the patients' emotional needs.

Let us return again to the individual categories. Among the aggression objects, the black giant bag seems to be of greatest importance, followed by the red giant block. When reading the patients' explanations to that end, the unrestricted expression of aggressions is actually the most important evaluation motif here. The patients described that anger could be released and touch-specific anxieties could be overcome by acting on the bag, if such anger or anxieties were related to a close reference person.

As for special symbolizing objects, it became obvious that they only gain in importance later. The individual reasons given by the patients are focus-oriented, usually specifically referring to their own work on a conflict. In addition, these reasons were stated several times especially by patients who very often worked with complex activity-specific performances.

As for the category of the dialogue contact objects, the stuffed animals used stand out because of the great importance attributed to them continuously. Stuffed animal dialogues, plays, and activity-specific explorations helped the patients, according to their own statements in the questionnaire, to better express themselves emotionally, to verbalize relationship problems and relationship wishes more directly in the transference with the therapist, and to find creative solutions for behavioral patterns that got stuck. In this context, stuffed animals were praised as objects with which the patients were able to communicate in an infantile way and to re-find a part of their familial world, i.e. also the disorder atmosphere of earlier times. In addition, model dialogues offered the playful opportunity to make up for something that had usually not been possible under the influence of the difficult parents: A resonance-capable, empathetic dialogue with statements, which may be withdrawn at any time, which can be tried out, or equipped with wishes, which an adult would otherwise express no longer directly.

This means that to me playing is one of the archetypical human forms of testing development and thus also a *founded psychotherapy*.

As for the category of special stabilization objects, it can be noted that these therapy objects ranked in third place in terms of the importance attributed to them based on the patients' experience. In the written explanations they were described among others as unrenounceable means for expressing the state of feeling sheltered in a relationship or as relaxing fun.

2. Therapy objects used in group settings

Here, the aim was to investigate whether different settings – this means, of course, the patients using these settings – reveal different tendencies with regard to the use of therapy objects.

For space reasons only the objects most often mentioned in the first statement of the group were taken into consideration.

Graph 12: Relevance of the objects in the group

Group A
a) closed group setting in addition
to the individual therapy setting

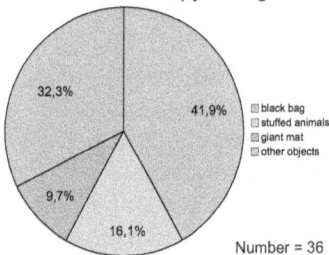

32,3%
41,9%
9,7%
16,1%

☐ black bag
☐ stuffed animals
☐ giant mat
☐ other objects

Number = 36

Group B
b) open course group setting in addition to the individual therapy setting

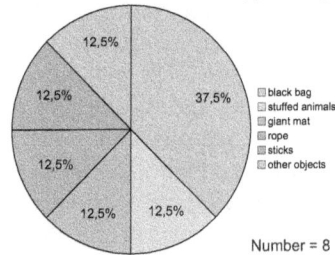

12,5%
12,5%
37,5%
12,5%
12,5%
12,5%

☐ black bag
☐ stuffed animals
☐ giant mat
☐ rope
☐ sticks
☐ other objects

Number = 8

Group C
trauma therapy setting

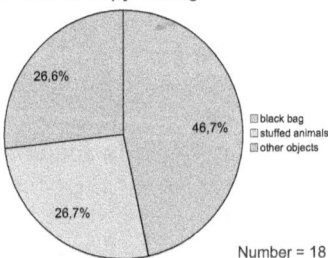

26,6%
46,7%
26,7%

☐ black bag
☐ stuffed animals
☐ other objects

Number = 18

Group D
individual therapy setting only

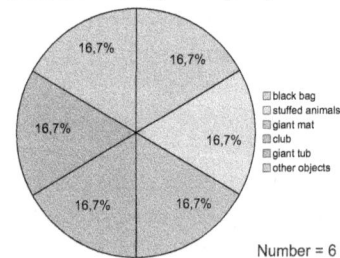

16,7%
16,7%
16,7%
16,7%
16,7%
16,7%

☐ black bag
☐ stuffed animals
☐ giant mat
☐ club
☐ giant tub
☐ other objects

Number = 6

These pie charts show that the helpful relevance of the black giant bag and of stuffed animals is especially high for patients with extensive structural activity-specific performances (groups A and C). There seems to be the tendency that the interplay between the aim to overcome anxieties and to express anger versus empathetic stuffed animal dialogues is especially very useful for patients with a trauma therapy setting; this is also suggested by the verbal explanations given by the patients.

The use of the therapy objects in the groups B and D seems to be less accentuated. Apart from the restriction that the groups were very small, one might hypothetically suggest that a rather equal use of therapy objects can be observed in less group-dynamic or individual-dynamic settings.

3. Therapy objects used under consideration of the experience of satisfaction and the therapy setting

Since the setting groups of the open course group (group B above) and the individual therapy group were very small, and since the evaluation structure of the use of therapy objects was quite similar, I put them together for the purpose of determining descriptive explanation and research hypotheses (group B plus D equalling a total of 14 persons, i.e. Number = 14 persons).

As a first question, I checked statistically whether the setting groups were distinguished by any differences concerning the therapy satisfaction they experienced.

This was not the case. In tendency only the patients of the group A and C were more satisfied with the psychotherapy they experienced and the external responses to the behavioral modifications on the part of the environment in comparison to the patients of the combined setting group B/D.

In another statistical data analysis, it was investigated whether the degree of the therapy satisfaction experienced or the perceived responses of the environment might perhaps be connected with the accentuated use of certain therapy objects.

To that end, satisfaction categories ranging from stages I to III were formed separately for all patients (Number = 50), who had completed a questionnaire regarding the patient's satisfaction, and the setting groups; these stages represent the following satisfaction experience:

- 0 to 50 % = stage 1 = little to moderately satisfied
- 60 to 70 % = stage 2 = generally satisfied
- *80 to 100 % = stage 3 = very satisfied*

On the basis of cross charts, the degree of satisfaction of all patients was then determined according to the three stages. Based on the Chi Square Test according to Pearson, it was revealed that patients who were generally satisfied and very satisfied with the therapy (stages 2 and 3) tended to mention the black giant bag significantly more often as relevant and useful in their first statement to question 12 (Chi Square Pearson: *(28, 924; df 22)*, asymptomic significance – both sides *(0.147)*). This was *48 % of the patients satisfied*. With regard to the second statement of question 12, it was noted that the patients satisfied (stages 2 and 3) tended more to appreciate the stuffed animals (Chi Square Pearson: *(27, 839; df 24)*; asymptomic significance – both sides *(0.267)*). This was almost 40 % of the patients satisfied.

Starting from the third statement, there were no longer any weighted allocations fields regarding the satisfaction groups.

Trying to investigate the background still further, the next question was, whether there had been a different order in stating the therapy objects used under question 12 in the setting subgroups, differentiated according to the stages of satisfaction with respect to question 1a.

Here, too, the well-known tendency could again be recognized, in that almost half up to about one third of the patients, who were rather more satisfied, always said that the black giant bag was the most important therapy object for them.

The more satisfied patients of these three setting groups also preferred the stuffed animals as their second most important object (scores around 20 %). The remainder was incidentally distributed among other objects. These comparisons are not yet of any significance statistically due to the small random samples or the wide range of variations of the answers.

4. Differences of the setting groups concerning the answers to questions 1 to 7 of the questionnaire regarding the patient's satisfaction

When comparing the setting groups as group A (Number = 36), group C (Number = 18), and group B/D (Number = 14) and reviewing in how far the tendencies of the answers given by these groups to the said questions differentiate from each other, then a Chi Square comparison (df = 2) leads to following significant result:

Table 20:

Question No.	Setting groups	N	M	SD	Chi² Test
3	Group A	36	63,78	21,78	4.88; p<0.08 (tendency)
	Group B/D	14	44,29	18,13	

Question No.	Setting groups	N	M	SD	Chi² Test
5b	Group A	36	66,76	22,86	8.42; p<0.05 significant
	Group B/D	14	38,57	17,73	
5d	Group A	36	64,66	24,89	7.14; p<0.05 significant
	Group B/D	14	37,14	25,64	
6b	Group A	36	67,57	19,35	5.27; p<0.05 significant
	Group B/D	14	44,29	24,39	
7a	Group A	36	45,59	23,89	1.95; p<0.05 significant
	Group C	18	58,75	18,21	

The chart shows that in connection with the subquestions 3, 5b, 5d, and 6b there was a significantly greater satisfaction of the patients' group with a closed group setting compared to the patients' group with an open group setting or an individual setting.

With regard to the questions this means that the result of group A reflects that it distinguishes itself by a more health-conscious behaviour due to the therapy, that the patients feel more satisfied in their social and partnership environments, and that they have the impression that their friends and acquaintances have also been more satisfied with them since the therapy work.

The discrepancy in satisfaction between the group of patients with a trauma setting and a closed setting shows, that the social environment of the trauma patients was possibly more satisfied with these patients prior to the therapy than in the case of other patients. If this were really true, it might be useful to explore the question, whether trauma patients without any treatment tend to be more adaptive due to their disorder than other individuals, or if they tend to become withdrawn as a consequence of the order.

The differences in the answers determined may, however, only be considered as a hypothesis, since no statistical group differences may generally be applied to the setting groups, and since it must also be reviewed, whether the more difficult patients were in fact in the course groups and individual therapy settings.

As treaters we know that we invite the patients first, against the background of the therapeutic process, to join course groups and that motivated patients are then very interested in joining a closed therapy group for a duration of two years with a total of eight therapy events (see 1.3.5 above). Therefore, it can clearly be evidenced that trauma patients and patients with a closed group setting make use of more therapeutic work within the same assessment time.

5. Evaluation of the individual answers to questions 13 to 16 of the questionnaire regarding the patient's satisfaction

These were open questions with respect to especially helpful interventions from the patient's point of view, the most joyous and the worst therapy situations, and the most important insights. The answers were not yet categorized within the framework of this first survey, because I would like to work out research hypotheses to that end first.

At the moment, I can therefore only describe the emotional impression the respective 50 answers made on me.

Question 13 asked which interventions the patient considered most helpful, based on three stages.

More than half of the 50 patients made positive comments on the psycho-educational introduction of the therapy and on the explanation of the diagnosis and treatment concepts in these three lines. According to the patients' statements, the therapists helped with these structurally-revealing interventions to relieve their relationship to the patient from a lot of feelings of guilt and also to make the patients conscious of their self-initiative. And the clear derivation of current behavioural ideas from the verbal therapeutic work also had a positive effect, according to the point of view of many patients.

Second ranking in the frequency of the statements were individual moments of the movement therapy, where patients praised a useful performance with the group or with the therapist. This referred both to work with specific objects (e.g. egg or rope) and to physical attention with hands or protective covers, etc. Next, accepting interpersonal dialogues were mentioned as helpful situations. Here, strong feelings of closeness due to a shared dismay and good verbalizations of diffuse affects were stressed.

Ranking in approximately the fourth line were hard clarifications of relationships (arguments, fees for sessions missed, etc.). The patients attributed about the same value to possible changes of the setting and some trauma-oriented interventions, which were considered as especially helpful. Another group of statements could not be classified; they refer to a number of trivialities such as the therapist's appearance, the look of the therapy room, the stipulation of session dates, birthdays, and the like.

After the efficiency of the intervention, question 14 simply asked for the most joyous situation. Here, the main tendency was that a great number of regressive group therapy scenes or individual body-oriented movement sessions were described, where childlike play had been great fun. The range of variation included a simple tug-of-war in the group, animal zoo plays with stuffed animals, building a hut for the group, and even birthday parties in the "nursery group". In individual therapy, such favorite scenes were joint gales of laughter between the patient and the therapist, a joint stuffed animal play, or an awkwardness of the therapist. The tendency of a very individual consideration of humor was also very high here (almost one third of the statements). Included in the list of such incidents were a funny phone conversation with a slip of the tongue, drumming on the therapist, the end of an argument, or a group therapy break with a big fancy cake, and the like.

In the case of question 15, the structures of the answers were still more wide-ranging.

The only tendency with respect to the worst or most horrible therapy situation were repeatedly-mentioned relationship tensions between the patient and the therapist. Again these referred to situations where the backgrounds of the fee regulation for missed sessions had been misunderstood, or to an affectively expressed feeling of the therapists, a residual feeling after a negative therapy experience, or a non-reachability of the therapists during a vacation. The remaining descriptions of any bad or horrible therapy experiences could not be categorized. For example, one patient mentioned an AIDS test invoking anxieties. Other ones described an embarrassing situation with fellow patients (nausea or bladder pressure). On the other hand, the patients also mentioned in this category those experiences where, within the framework of a therapy session, they had suddenly become aware of a sexual abuse in their childhood at home or as a scene of violence in the EMDR.

Question 16 aimed at clarifying the relevance of the most important insight or achievement. More than half of the patients mentioned important self-experiences here, which had led to a more adult view of a problem, a more adult competence to resolve conflicts, and to a healthier self-responsibility. The patients often described situations, which had been correlated both in the individual or group therapy and in practical life, and which could be easily transformed.

As for the contents, the tendency of the answers with respect to the patient's satisfaction recalled the answers given to questions 1 to 7, because it became evident in which area the patients most appreciated their positive modifications.

In the last category, messages to the therapists, wishes, confirmations, and proposals for improvements were noted.

It became clear that patients needed and appreciated comprehensible structures and good relationships. They wanted an extension of the group experience again and again, and considered it important that the therapists were actively involved in the body dialogue. An emotional expression of great anger and of hilarious humor was also often stressed and desired in the extension.

3.2 Hypotheses and Objectives for Further Research of Effects

Due to the results indicated in 3.1 above, positive treatment results could be supported in terms of a quantitative and qualitative confirmation.

The use of standardized diagnostic procedures should, however, be increased, so that other comparisons of random samples are made possible and can be extended purposefully.

To that end, Krampen's STEP (2002) as well as Richter's and Guthke's LEBI (1996) could be used, so that the therapist's experience would be more fully recorded together with the patient's experience in a specific therapy session, or so that standardized comparative values could be used for a qualitative assessment of life events in connection with a pre/post-comparison at the time of any therapy changes.

The results of the structural universal psychotherapy indicate at the moment, that patients with whom a flexible therapy and relationship setting is possible, experience within a short holistic changes of their behavioral and relationship structures.

The combination of individual and group therapy seems to be particularly effective, especially if the patients' group works as a closed community with self-help structures.

In this context, more research is still required in order to investigate, which patients get greater opportunities for change in precisely this combination, and why, and what is the particularity of the therapeutic relationship, if patients are not suitable for this path. In group therapy, which generally helps to develop and to specify the problem of a wide range of social and individual changes, the paths of individual psycho-dynamic modification processes should still be represented in more detail and in an experience-nearer way, i. e. especially in terms of the reflection of the participants concerned.

Unfortunately, there are only a few manageable inventories available for process diagnostics, which are also economically and organizationally acceptable under the conditions of a walk-in practice. A more individual process diagnostics would also include a differentiated representation of the specific therapy development of diagnosis groups in a pre/post-comparison. In this context, it would be important to include the problem of a better and more complex consideration of external criteria in any scientific consideration.

4 Appendix

4.1 Photographs of the Therapy Objects Used

Appendix to 1.3.1.1 – Category: Representation of the transitional transference objects

Photo 1:Red giant block

Photo 2: Red giant block during a performance

Photo 3: Black giant limp bag

Photo 4: Black giant limp bag during a performance

Photo 5: White wall

Photo 6: White wall during a performance

Photo 7: Green giant mat

Photo 8: Green giant mat during a performance

Photo 9: Giant tub

Photo 10: Giant tub during a performance

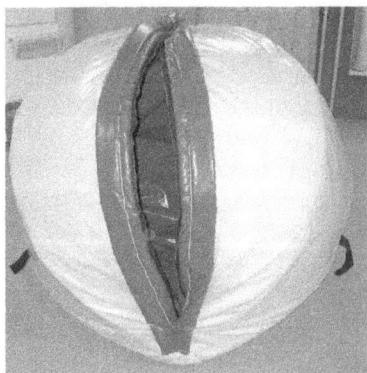

Photo 11: Giant egg

Photo 12: Giant egg during a performance

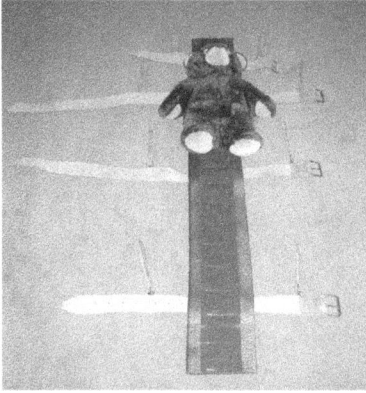

Photo 13: Hover belt

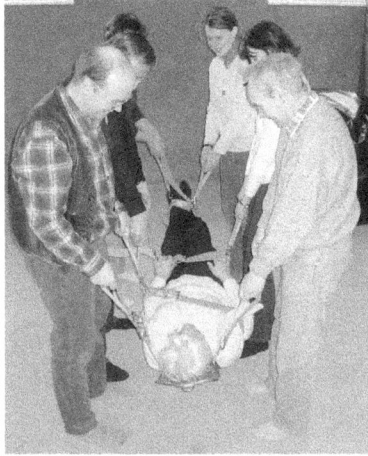

Photo 14: Hover belt
during a performance

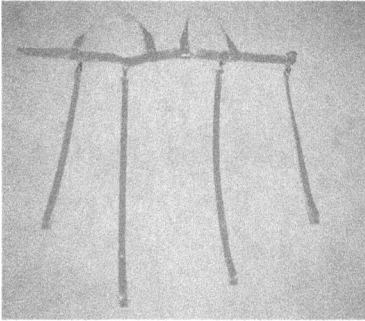

Photo 15: Harnesses

Photo 16: Harnesses
during a performance

Photo 17: Clubs

Photo 18: Clubs during
a performance

Photo 19: Group rope
during a performance

Photo 20: Group rope
during a performance

Photo 21: Hammock
during a performance

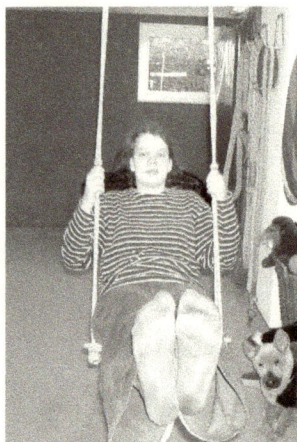

Photo 22: Swing during
a performance

Photo 23: Yellow bag
during a performance

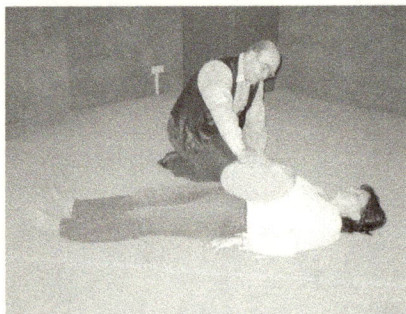

Photo 24: Belly pillow
during a performance

Photo 25: Swinging bag during a performance

Photo 26: Fingerball during a performance

Photo 27: Blanket during a performance

Photo 28: Sticks during a performance

Photo 29: Stuffed animals during a performance

Photo 30: Stuffed animals during a performance

4.2 Table of Pictures of Selected Drawings and Sculptures Referring to Case Examples of Patients

Appendix to 1.3.4 – Category:
Therapy drawings

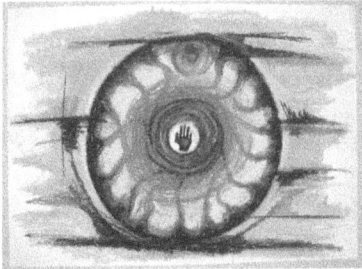

Developmental Survey of the Drawings of Patient B

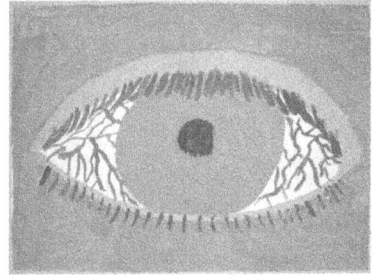

Photo 31: Patient A

Photo 34: Drawing B-1

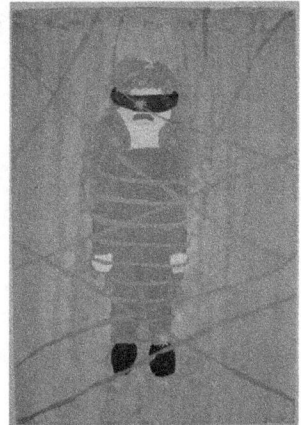

Photo 32: Patient B

Photo 36: Drawing B-3 (left)

Photo 35: Drawing B-2

Photo 33: Patient C

Photo 37: Drawing B-4

Photo 38: Drawing B-5

Therapeutic Contact Shelf

Photo 39: Drawing B-5

Photo 40: Contact shelf in the conversation room

Therapy Figures
Patient D

Photo 41: Sculpture D-1

Photo 42: Sculpture D-2

Photo 43: Sculpture D-3

Patient E

Photo 44: Sculpture E-1

Photo 45: Sculpture E-2

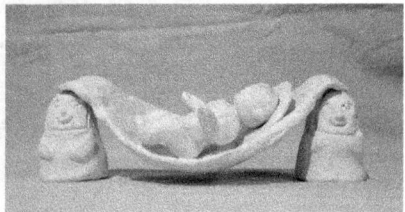

Photo 46: Sculpture E-3

Patient F

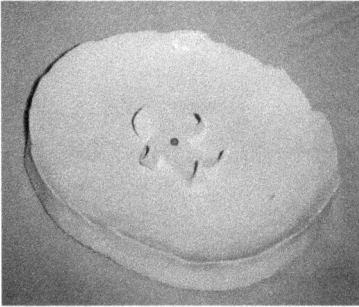

Photo 47: Sculpture F-1

Photo 48: Sculpture F-2

Photo 49: Sculpture F-3

Patient Detlef Heinel

Photo 50: Sculpture H-1

Photo 51: Sculpture H-2

Photo 52: Sculpture H-3

Photo 53: Sculpture H-4

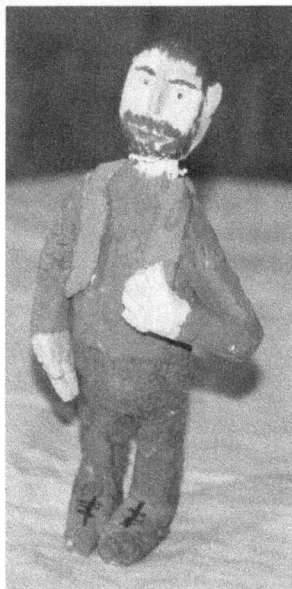

Photo 54: Sculpture H-5

Photo 55: Sculpture H-6

4.3 Explanations of Terms Relating to the Concept of a Structural Universal Psychotherapy

This survey explains how important conceptual terms of this book are to be used and have been developed.

1. Transference
A neurotic form of an acquired self-regulation.

Unconsciously or consciously, and unavoidably, behavioural patterns which developed in terms of a reciprocal effect with psychically stressful reference persons and/or life events are reproduced here. In this connection, the individual either tries to re-use the behavioural patterns he or she acquired, or to counteract the effect of the reciprocal structure he or she experienced, in terms of the previous survival strategy or of the previous success of dealing with the situation.

Transferences are triggered by conditions of the reflected external and internal world of the individual which are psychically perceived as being similar.

Transferences may therefore occur as an absolute weakness of differentiation, as a partial misinterpretation, or as an excessive response to a real psychic problem situation. The majority of the transferences are associated with a noticeable restriction of other behavioral competences in terms of individual relapses and/or a clear restriction of the ability to learn with respect to new and modified reciprocal structures in the form of reactive blockades.

This means, that transferences inhibit the development of adult regulation structures and keep the individual in the dependency of reference persons and/or damaging situations, who and/or which were previously experienced as impairing.

2. Introject
A neurotic form of an acquired self-regulation.

Unconsciously or consciously, and unavoidably, behavioural patterns which developed in terms of a reciprocal effect with psychically stressful reference persons and/or life events are produced and reproduced here. In terms of an adoption of the previously experienced (i.e. observed and/or suffered) behavioral patterns the individual tries to use these shaping reciprocal structures in order to increase or to stabilize his control of his own behavior or of situations. The introjected regulation patterns are used to control the structures of the psychic conditions of the internal and external world.

Introjects may thus be seen as absolute identifications with formerly impairing forces, as a partial imitation of the influence experienced, or as a latent acting out in terms of the previously shaping power and situation.

Introjects are internalized and strengthened by subliminal model learning and by a considerable negative selective and/or long-term psychic pressure (extreme stress). They intervene especially actively in the current regulation of the individual's behaviour, when the individual would like to deal better with an inner-psychic tension, which he or she experiences as ambivalent (urge for a successful extension of identity) short-term. On the other hand, introjects are also especially noticeable, when a loosening of old behavioral structures is associated with too heavy risks of failure, so that relief is sought in well-known stereotypes (fear or shame of a loss of identity).

This means, that introjects interfere, in particular, with the formation of any new, independent, distinguishable structures, so that the connection to the previously impairing reference persons and/or damaging situation is maintained.

3. Introject Transference Chart

A psychotherapeutic means of work for the patient and the therapist being used to represent *shaping psycho-dynamic* partial forces, in order to be able to derive hypotheses with regard to the psychic reciprocal conflicts of the functional self-regulation disorder. The contents of the work charts is always related to the respective status of the therapy, the patient's verbalization level, and the dynamic of resistance and defense being made aware at the moment.

Depending on the phase of the therapy, the hypothetical assessments of the patient and of the therapist are more or less different and are combined to a joint working hypothesis (focus), from which specific solution proposals for the therapeutic performance and evaluation work are to be derived.

4. Transitional Transference Objects

Transitional transference objects are therapy objects which are used to symbolize inner-psychic problems within the framework of structural activity-specific performances during therapeutic work.

These therapy objects possess qualities of larger or smaller psychically vaguely associatively and emotionally laden impressions, which can accelerate this psychotherapeutic work; this triangulating object provides the therapist with the possibility of supplementing any difficult transference sides with these objects, and to work together with the patient on a reduction of these transferences.

A therapeutic transitional transference object is explicitly and selectively created by its intended and indicated use, the "beseelte" experience quality of the patient in a specific psycho-dynamic process, and the final extensive reduction or reduceability of the psychic regressive atmosphere by the patient with the support of the therapist.

5. Introject Transference Role Play

A role play setting, where a model for inner-psychic regulation possibilities is to be diagnostically demonstrated and worked on therapeutically.

The core of the patient's active self-confrontation is that he or she penetrates the functional reciprocity of his or her acquired transference and introject sides, in order to modify them in terms of a healthier, independent self-regulation.

6. Introject Generation Role Play

A role play setting, where a model for inner-familial regulation scripts extending to three generations is to be demonstrated and worked on therapeutically.

The core of the patient's more active self-involvement is that he or she learns to better understand how the functional relationships between the transference and introject side he or she experiences are penetrated by the psychic introject experiences of his or her parents as children of their parents (grandparents) or of any important reference persons, and to find selectively and uniquely a model-like solution for their neurosis context, whereby in turn his or her own psychic detachment will be enhanced.

7. Structural Activity-Specific Performances

Structural activity-specific performances are relationship and behavioral models, which serve to actively demonstrate and work on any disordered or non-adequately developed experience and activity regulations of the patient. Such performances can be used to enhance the patient's psychic resources, to treat any derived conflicts, or for an experimental exploration of the patient's self-regulation.

The patient, the therapist, and/or the therapy group usually work in a mutual relationship-based way cooperatively together, after having discussed, substantiated, negotiated, and diagnostically or in a solution-oriented way aligned together the explosive effect and the objective of the setting.

8. Mutual Relationship-Based Procedure

By analogy with Ferenczi (1932), this refers to an interpersonal relationship between the patient and the therapist, where on the basis of a worked out equality, a similar risk of spontaneity, of depth and of resonance capacity, both sides allow an interpersonal reciprocity for the purpose of a therapeutically indicated joint action.

There is, however, a certain difference compared to Ferenczi's definition. As I use the term, it does not refer to a complete exchange of roles between the patient and therapist, but only to an above-average, spontaneous transparency and a quick readiness to act in the current relationship and activity-specific dialogue. In this connection, the therapist and, if possible, the patient, too, will be active both in a conscious therapeutic dissociation from any reflecting adult psychic structures and in spontaneously acting infantile or intuitively archaic structures.

9. Body Movement Orientation
Here, this means that usually after the verbal analysis of the relationship and behavior, a therapeutic body movement sequence is derived to illustrate or to treat the disorder structure. This body movement sequence tries to achieve for the patient and for the therapist a physical diagnostic review of the context discussed and/or a physical behavioral solution as a possible preliminary stage of the modification of the self-regulation strived for.

10. Trauma Orientation
Here, this means that important insights of modern psychotraumatology are taken into consideration. This refers both to the diagnostic approach when it comes to the investigation of any wide, branched disorder causes and deficiencies in terms of any complex and multiple disorders, and to the therapeutic work with a flexible and – if possible and important – little relationship-dynamizing setting.

The treatment strategies of psychotraumatology may also be found in a role-play-like breakdown of any inner parts of a personality, in an understanding of a strengthening of resources, and in dealing with triggers in the therapeutic process.

Experimental psychotherapeutic activity-specific performances often lead back to traumatized experience points in the patient's self-experience, which are sometimes of key importance for the behavioral modification strived for.

11. Universal Psychotherapy
This is a general term referring to the integrated – partially very differently aligned – therapy approaches in this concept. The term is to indicate, that the approach of the structural activity-specific performances may vice versa also be fertile for the integrated therapy models. In addition, the term "universal" implies here the meaning of being easily manageable for the patient and the accordingly trained therapist, of being flexibly broken up into the individual therapy elements, and of being useable in a wide range of individual and group therapies.

4.4 Sources of Proven Therapy Objects

Vogt & Vogt – Objekte GbR

Therapeutic Auxiliary Objects
For children and adults
To be used for structural activity-specific
performances in psychotherapy

Contact: Dr. rer. Nat. Ralf Vogt and
Irina Vogt, MD - Psychology
Leipziger Str. 36 a, D-04178 Leipzig
kontakt@vogt-objekte.de

Seminars are offered to get acquainted with the
manifold possibilities of applications and the respective
indications. Please contact us for more information.
Phone number: +49-(0)341-4429129
Office hours: Monday to Friday 9 am – 12 am
www.vogt-objekte.de • www.leipzigerakademie.de

4.5 Bibliography

ARNOLD, W.; EYSENCK, H. J.; MEILI, R. (1993): Lexikon der Psychologie. vol. 1 – 3, Freiburg: Herder, 11th edition.

BALINT, M. (Editor, 1936): Schriften zur Psychoanalyse: Sandor Ferenczi. Frankfurt/M.: Fischer, 2 vol.
BALINT, M. (1970): Therapeutische Aspekte der Regression. Die Theorie der Grundstörung. Stuttgart: Klett-Cotta; The Basic Fault: Therapeutic Aspects of Regression, London, 1968.
BECKER, H. (1997): Konzentrative Bewegungstherapie – Integrationsversuch von Körperlichkeit und Handeln im psychoanalytischen Prozeß. Gießen: Psychosozial-Verlag, 2nd edition (2001).
BETTIGHOFER, S. (1998): Übertragung und Gegenübertragung im therapeutischen Prozeß. Stuttgart: Kohlhammer, 2. Aufl. (2000).
BION, W. R. (1971): Erfahrungen in Gruppen und andere Schriften. Stuttgart: Klett-Cotta; Experiences in Groups, New York, 1961.
BOADELLA, D. C. (1991): Befreite Lebensenergie, Einführung in die Biosynthese. München: Kösel.
BOCIAN, B.; STAEMMLER, F.-M. (Hrsg.) (2000): Gestalttherapie und Psychoanalyse. Göttingen: Vandenhoeck & Ruprecht.

CLAUSS, G.; EBNER, H. (1974): Grundlagen der Statistik. Berlin: Volk und Wissen.

DORNES, M. (1997): Die frühe Kindheit. Frankfurt/M.: Fischer.
DORNES, M. (1998): Der kompetente Säugling. Frankfurt/M.: Fischer, 8th edition.
DORNES, M. (2000): "Affektspiegelung – Zur symbol- und identitätsbildenden Funktion früher Interaktion". In: STREECK (editor): Erinnern, Agieren und Inszenieren. Göttingen: Vandenhoeck & Ruprecht.
DORNES, M. (2002 a): "Ist die Kleinkindforschung irrelevant für die Psychoanalyse?" In: Psyche, No. 56, pp. 888 – 921.
DORNES, M (2002 b): "Menschenbilder in Psychoanalyse und Säuglingsforschung: Konflikt oder Dialog?" Unpublished Lecture at the 3rd Vienna Symposium "Psychoanalysis and Body", Vienna, September 27/28, 2002.
DOWNING, G. (1996): Körper und Wort in der Psychotherapie. München: Kösel; The Body and the Word. A Direction for Psychotherapy, 1996.

DÜHRSSEN, A. (1962): "Katamnestische Ergebnisse bei 1004 Patienten nach analytischer Psychotherapie". In: Psychosomatische Medizin, No. 10, pp. 94 – 113.

DÜHRSSEN, A; JORSWIECK, E. (1965): "Untersuchung zur Leistungfähigkeit psychoanalytischer Behandlung". In: Nervenarzt, No. 36 (1965), pp. 166 – 169.

ERMANN, M. (1994): "Sandor Ferenczis Aufbruch und Scheitern. Sein Umgang mit der Regression aus heutiger Sicht". In: Psyche, 48, No. 8, pp. 706 – 719.

FERENCZI, S. (1921): "Weiterer Ausbau der 'aktiven Technik' in der Psychoanalyse". In: Ferenczi, S. (1964) Bausteine zur Psychoanalyse, vol. II, Stuttgart: Huber, 2nd edition; "Further Extension of the Active Technique in Psychoanalysis", 1920; in: The Fundamentals of Psychoanalysis, 1939.

FERENCZI, S. (1928): "Die Elastizität der psychoanalytischen Technik". In: Ferenczi, S. (1964) Bausteine zur Psychoanalyse, vol. III, Stuttgart: Huber, 2nd edition; "The Elasticity of Psychoanalytic Technique"; in: The Fundamentals of Psychoanalysis, 1939.

FERENCZI, S. (1931): "Kinderanalysen mit Erwachsenen". In: Ferenczi, S. (1964): Bausteine zur Psychoanalyse. Vol. III, Stuttgart: Huber, 2nd edition; "Child Analysis in the Analysis of Adults", 1931; in: The Fundamentals of Psychoanalysis, 1939.

FERENCZI, S. (1932): "Sprachverwirrung zwischen den Erwachsenen und dem Kind". In: Ferenczi, S. (1964): Bausteine zur Psychoanalyse. vol. III, Stuttgart: Huber, 2nd edition; "Confusion of Tongues between Adult and Child", 1949; in: The Fundamentals of Psychoanalysis.

FERENCZI, S. (1964): Bausteine zur Psychoanalyse. Vol. I to III, Stuttgart: Huber, 2nd edition; The Fundamentals of Psychoanalysis, 1939.

FERENCZI, S. (1988): Ohne Sympathie keine Heilung. Das klinische Tagebuch von 1932. Frankfurt/M.: Suhrkamp; The Clinical Diary of Sandor Ferenczi, 1988.

FORTUNE, CH. (1994): "Der Fall 'R. N.' Sandor Ferenczi radikales psychoanalytisches Experiment". In: Psyche, 48, No. 8, pp. 683 – 703; "The Case of 'RN' Sandor Ferencizi's Radical Psychoanalytic Experiment".

FRANKE, G. H. (2000): Brief Symptom Inventory von L. R. Derogatis (Kurzform der SCL-90-R), Göttingen: Beltz Test GmbH.

FREUD, S. (1920): Jenseits des Lustprinzips. In: Gesammelte Werke, (1969), vol. XIII; Beyond the Pleasure Principle, SE, vol. 18, pp. 7 – 64.

FREUD, S. (1969): Ges. Werke, vol. I – XVIII, Zur Ätiologie der Hysterie; vol. I, pp. 423 – 459, Frankfurt/Main: Fischer, 3rd edition; On the Etyology of Hysteria, SE, vol. 3, pp. 189 – 221.

GEISSLER, P. (Editor, 1998): Analytische Körperpsychotherapie in der Praxis. München: Pfeiffer, Klett-Cotta.

GEISSLER, P. (2001): Mythos Regression. Gießen: Psychosozial-Verlag.

GEISSLER, P. (2002): "Psychoanalyse und Körper: Überlegungen zum gegenwärtigen Stand analytischer Körperpsychotherapie". In: Psychoanalyse und Körper. 1, No.1, pp. 37 – 81.

GEISSLER, P. (2003): Körperbilder. Collected Writings presented on occasion of the 3rd Vienna Symposium "Psychoanalysis and Body". Gießen: Psychosozial-Verlag.

GRAWE, K.; DONATI, R.; BERNAUER, F. (1994): Psychotherapie im Wandel. Von der Konfession zur Profession. Göttingen: Hogrefe.

GUTHKE, J. (1996): Intelligenz im Test: Wege der psychologischen Intelligenzdiagnostik. Göttingen: Vandenhoeck & Ruprecht.

HEINRICH, V. (2001): "Übertragungs- u. Gegenübertragungsbeziehung in der Körperpsychotherapie". In: Psychotherapie Forum, No. 9, pp. 62 – 70.

HEISTERKAMP, G. (1993): Heilsame Berührungen. München: Pfeiffer.

HEISTERKAMP, G. (1999): "Zur Freude in der analytischen Psychotherapie". In: Psyche, No. 53, pp. 1247-1265.

HENNIG, H. (Editor) (1999): Katathym – imaginative Psychotherapie als analytischer Prozeß. Lengerich: Pabst.

HESSEL, A.; SCHUMACHER, J.; GEYER, M.; BRÄHLER, E. (2001): "Symptom-Checkliste SCL-90-R: Testtheoretische Überprüfung und Normierung an einer bevölkerungsrepräsentativen Stichprobe". In: Diagnostica, No. 47/1, pp. 27 – 39.

HOFMANN, A. (1999): EMDR in der Therapie psychotraumatischer Belastungssyndrome. Stuttgart: Thieme.

HUBER, M. (2003 a): Trauma und die Folgen. Trauma und Traumabehandlung. Part 1. Paderborn: Junfermann.

HUBER, M. (2003 b): Wege der Traumabehandlung. Trauma und Traumabehandlung. Part 2. Paderborn: Junfermann.

KLEIN, M. (1932): Die Psychoanalyse des Kindes. Wien: Internat. Psychoanalyse Verlag; The Psychoanalysis of Children, New York, 1927.

KLEIN, M. (1962): Das Seelenleben des Kleinkindes und andere Beiträge zur

Psychoanalyse. Stuttgart: Klett-Cotta.

KOEMEDA-LUTZ, M. (2003): "Zwischenergebnisse zur Wirksamkeit von ambulanten Körperpsychotherapien". In: Psychotherapie Forum, No. 11, pp. 70 – 79.

KÖNIG, O. (2003): "Ein unmöglicher Beruf: Zur Professionalisierung der Gruppendynamik". In: Gruppenpsychother. Gruppendynamik, 39, No. 3, pp. 261 – 277.

VAN DER KOLK, B. A.; MC FARLANE, A. C.; WEISAETH, L. (2000): Traumatic Stress. Paderborn: Junfermann.

KRAMPEN, G. (2002): STEP, Stundenbogen für die Allgemeine und Differentielle Einzelpsychotherapie. Göttingen: Hogrefe.

LACHAUER, R. (1992): Der Focus in der Psychotherapie. München: Pfeiffer, Klett-Cotta. 1999, 2nd edition.

LAPLANCHE, J.; PONTALIS, J. B. (1991): Das Vokabular der Psychoanalyse. Frankfurt/ M.: Suhrkamp, 10the edition; The Language of Psychoanalysis, New York, 1973.

LEVINE, P. A. (1998): Trauma-Heilung. Das Erwachen des Tigers. Essen: Synthesis-Verlag; Waking the Tiger. Healing Trauma, 1997.

LICHTENBERG, J. D. (1991): Psychoanalyse und Säuglingsforschung. Berlin: Springer.

LIENERT, G. A. (1969): Testaufbau und Testanalyse. Weinheim: Beltz. 3rd edition.

LOHSE, H.; LUDWIG, R.; RÖHR, M. (1986): Statistische Verfahren für Psychologen, Pädagogen und Soziologen. Berlin: Volk und Wissen, 2nd edition.

MAAZ, H.-J. (1997): Psychodynamische Einzeltherapie. Lengerich: Pabst.

MÄRTENS, M.; PETZOLD, H. (Editors, 2002): Therapieschäden. Risiken und Nebenwirkungen von Psychotherapie. Mainz: Matthias-Grünewald-Verlag.

MAHLER, M. S.; PINE, F.; BERGMANN, A. (1980): Die psychische Geburt des Menschen. Frankfurt/M.: Fischer, 16th edition (1999).

MERTENS, W. (1993): Einführung in die psychoanalytische Therapie. Vol. 1 – 3. Stuttgart: Kohlhammer, 2nd edition.

MORENO, J. L. (1946): Psychodrama. New York.

MOSER, T. (1987): Der Psychoanalytiker als sprechende Attrappe. Frankfurt/M.: Suhrkamp.

PESSO, A. (1986): Dramaturgie des Unbewußten. Stuttgart: Klett-Cotta, 2nd edition (1999).

PETZOLD, H.; SIEPER, J. (1996): Integration und Kreation, 2 vol., Paderborn: Junfermann.

POHLEN, M.; BAUTZ-HOLZHERR, M. (1995). Psychoanalyse – das Ende einer Deutungsmacht. Reinbek b. Hamburg: Rowohlt TB-Verlag.

RACKER, H. (1959): Übertragung und Gegenübertragung. München: Reinhardt.

RICHTER, V.; GUTHKE, J. (1996): Leipziger Ereignis- und Belastungsinventar (LEBI). Göttingen: Hogrefe.

SCHULTE, D. (1993): "Wie soll Therapieerfolg gemessen werden?"; in: Zeitschrift für Klinische Psychologie, No. 22/4, pp. 374 – 397.

SMUCKER, M. (2003): "Cognitive Behavioral Treatment for Adult Survivors of Childhood Trauma". Milwaukee, unpublished manuscript, seminar, Leipzig 2003.

STERN, D. N. (1991): Tagebuch eines Babys. München: Piper, 8th edition (2000); Diary of a Baby, New York, 1990.

STERN, D. N. (1996): Die Lebenserfahrung des Säuglings. Stuttgart: Klett-Cotta, 5th edition; The Interpersonal World of the Infant, New York, 1985.

VOGT, R. (2001a): "Analytische multimodale Körperpsychotherapie mit Übergangs-Übertragungs-Objekten als Symbolisierungsmedien". In TRAUTMANN-VOIGT, S.; VOIGT, B.: Bewegung und Bedeutung. Köln: C. Richter, pp. 112 – 132.

VOGT, R. (2001b): "Zum Einsatz und zur Konstruktion von Übergangs-Übertragungs-Objekten als Symbolisierungsmedien in der analytisch-multimodalen Körperpsychotherapie". In MAAZ, H.-J.; KRÜGER, A.: Integration des Körpers in die analytische Psychotherapie. Lengerich: Pabst, pp. 97 – 141.

VOGT, R. (2001c): "Zur körpertherapeutischen Regressionsförderung mit Übergangs-Übertragungs-Objekten". In: Forum der Bioenergetischen Analyse. No. 1, pp. 47 – 79.

VOGT, R. (2001d): "Übergangs-Übertragungs-Objekte in der multimodalen analytischen Körperpsychotherapie". In BAHRKE, U.; ROSENDAHL, W.: Psychotraumatologie und Katathym-imaginative Psychotherapie. Lengerich: Pabst, pp. 447 – 468.

VOGT, R. (2001e): "Fallvignetten zur Arbeit mit Übergangs-Übertragungs-Objekten". In: Forum der Bioenergetischen Analyse. No. 2, pp. 51 – 66.

VOGT, R. (2002a): "Beseelte Spielräume durch Übergangs-Übertragungs-

Objekte" In: Trautmann-voigt, S.; Voigt, B.: Verspieltheit als Ent-
wicklungschance. Gießen: Psychosozialverlag, pp. 173 – 208.

Vogt, R. (2002b): "Veränderung und Lösung von Übertragungsbarrieren in
der analytischen Körperpsychotherapie durch den Einsatz von Übergangs-Übertragungs-Objekten". In: Psychotherapie Forum, No. 10, pp.
22 – 37.

Vogt, R. (2002c): "Veränderung und Lösung von Übertragungsbarrieren in
der analytischen Körperpsychotherapie durch den Einsatz von Übergangs-Übertragungs-Objekten". In: Psychotherapie Forum, No. 10, pp.
22 – 37.

Vogt, R. (2003): "Beseelbare Objekte zur analytischen prozeßnahen
Handlungsdiagnostik und –therapie im körperpsychotherapeutischen
Setting – Fallvignetten zum methodischen Vorgehen". In: Psychoanalyse
und Körper, 2, pp. 41 – 58.

Watkins, J. G.; Watkins, H. H. (2003): Ego-States – Theorie und Therapie.
Heidelberg: Auer; Ego States – Theory and Therapy, 1978.

Winnicott, D. (1974): Reifungsprozesse und fördernde Umwelt. München:
Kindler; Maturational Processes and the Facilitating Environment.

Wollschläger, M.-E. u. Wollenschläger, G (1998): Der Schwan und
die Spinne. Bern: Hans Huber.

Psychosozial-Verlag

Vita Heinrich-Clauer (Ed.)
Handbook Bioenergetic Analysis

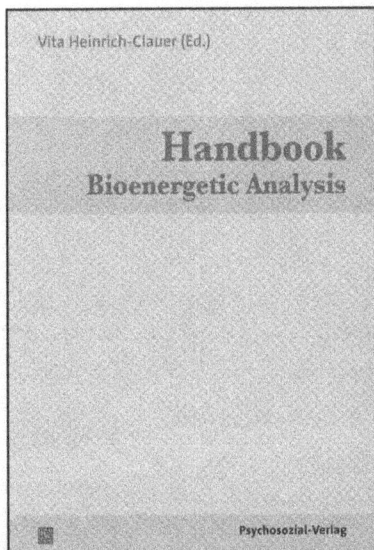

The more recent articles connect the concepts of relational psychoanalysis with the findings from emotion and infant research, attachment theory as well as neurobiology. The integration of implicit knowing and the importance for including the body in the therapy process is evident in these articles.

The articles demonstrate the broad spectrum of the prevailing concepts and profound therapeutic modalities of Bioenergetic Analysis. Case studies illustrate the concepts and provide practical relevance.

Central themes of the book are: the Self in relation with others, sexuality and love, trauma, psychosomatics as well as the conceptual discussion of the therapeutic process. Studies on effectiveness of Bioenergetic Analysis and body psychotherapy in general complete the spectrum.

2011 · 539 Pages · Softcover
ISBN 978-3-8379-2102-1

This book is a selection of articles from Bioenergetic Analysis, that range from classical studies written in the Eighties (following Lowen) up to current theoretical contributions and case studies.

Walltorstr. 10 · 35390 Gießen · Tel. 0641-969978-18 · Fax 0641-969978-19
bestellung@psychosozial-verlag.de · www.psychosozial-verlag.de

www.ingramcontent.com/pod-product-compliance
Lightning Source LLC
Chambersburg PA
CBHW020354270326
41926CB00007B/431